ECLECTIC SERIES OF SCHOOL BOOKS.

The Eclectic Series has been undertaken by a few untiring laborers in the cause of education, for the purpose of furnishing a complete, *uniform* and *improved* set of school books, commencing with the alphabet. The books are commended by intelligent teachers.

ARITHMETICAL COURSE.

Ray's Eclectic Arithmetic, on the inductive and analytic methods of instruction. Designed for common schools and academies. By Joseph Ray, Professor of Mathematics in Woodward College, and late Teacher of Arithmetic in that Institution. Stereotyped.

Ray's Little Arithmetic, containing intellectual exercises for young beginners, and designed to precede the "Eclectic Arithmetic." Prepared expressly for the Eclectic Series. Stereotyped.

Ray's Tables and Rules in Arithmetic. For young children. Prepared for the Eclectic Series. Stereotyped.

This system of Arithmetic is the result of many years' labor, which the author entered upon (in compliance with the earnest solicitation of many friends of education,) with a view of preparing a *standard* work which would justify *general* use in schools. The effort has proved completely successful. The ease and rapidity with which even very young pupils can learn arithmetic from these books is highly gratifying. The author is a practical, ingenious and successful teacher. He has instructed children and youth of all ages and grades; and well knows what a school book ought to be.

READING COURSE.

The Eclectic Readers, by Mr. McGuffey (advertised on the back cover of this volume), were much needed. They have already been widely introduced into schools of the city and country. Numerous instructors, who are *practically* acquainted with their merits, from having *used* them with great success in teaching, pronounce them unequaled aids to the young learner, in this important branch of primary education. *Forty thousand* copies of these Readers have been sold in a few months.

THE

ECLECTIC SECOND READER;

CONSISTING OF

PROGRESSIVE LESSONS

IN

READING AND SPELLING.

FOR THE

YOUNGER CLASSES IN SCHOOLS.

WITH ENGRAVINGS.

BY WILLIAM H. McGUFFEY,
Professor in Miami University, Oxford

— 1836 —

CINCINNATI:
PUBLISHED BY TRUMAN AND SMITH
150 MAIN STREET

ROMAN NUMERALS EXPLAINED.

A numeral is a symbol meaning number. Our system of counting is believed to have begun by people counting on their fingers. Both the Arabic (1, 2, 3, 4, etc.) and the Roman (I, II, III, IV, etc.) are believed to have started this way. The word digit, meaning number, is from the Latin word digitus, meaning finger. The number V (5) seems to be representative of an open hand; and, the number X (10) seems to be like two open hands.

In earlier days, our forefathers used the Roman system to indicate chapter headings in books. To help you understand those numbers more easily you may refer to the chart below:

Roman	Arabic	Roman	Arabic	Roman	Arabic
I	1	XI	11	XXX	30
II	2	XII	12	XL	40
III	3	XIII	13	L	50
IV	4	XIV	14	LX	60
V	5	XV	15	LXX	70
VI	6	XVI	16	LXXX	80
VII	7	XVII	17	XC	90
VIII	8	XVIII	18	C	100
IX	9	XIX	19	D	500
X	10	XX	20	M	1000

Entered according to Act of Congress, in the year 1836
By TRUMAN & SMITH,
In the Clerk's Office for the District Court of Ohio.

ISBN 0-88062-003-X
Printed in the United States of America

PRESENT PUBLISHER'S PREFACE.

Out-of-print for over 125 years, the *original* McGuffey's Eclectic Readers are considered educational classics. These books are world renowned for their teaching of reading through the integration of faith with learning.

William Holmes McGuffey, outstanding 19th century educator and preacher, combined both of his God-given talents in the preparation of these early textbooks. Millions of copies were sold in their *original* Christ-centered form. The character of our Nation was molded in an upright manner through the repeated use of these textbooks over several generations.

In order to capture the true spirit of the *original* McGuffey's Eclectic Readers we have made no major content changes. While this edition of the *authentic* Readers is being presented in a more easily readable form, the stories, poems, and pictures appear as they did in the first edition.

Slight changes have taken place for the sake of clarification. Those changes are as follows: a. some punctuation has been changed to keep it consistent with current usage; b. the hyphen has been removed from words in the spelling exercises; c. the spelling of words has been brought up-to-date; and d. the following words have been changed - kinsmen to relatives, passion to mood, servant to mother, particulars to details, amiable to good, wished to wanted, shores to land, and brethren to relatives.

The Publisher wishes to express his heart-felt appreciation to the staff of the Special Collections Library at Miami University, Oxford, Ohio, for its cooperation in researching the *authenticity* of this book. Additionally, we desire to thank Dr. John H. Westerhoff, III, for his inspiration in promoting the republishing of the *original* works and Bohn Printing for their untiring efforts in typesetting the Readers.

It is indeed an honor and distinct pleasure to return the *original* McGuffey's Eclectic Readers to you. The content of this series will help you develop outstanding reading skills, Christ-centered character, a love for good literature, and impressive speaking abilities. I am sure you will find the *original* McGuffey's Eclectic Readers to be a valuable teaching tool whether they are used in the public school, Christian school, or for those who choose to teach their children at home.

George M. Mott, President
MOTT MEDIA, INC.

PREFACE.

This little book is designed, as its title indicates, to succeed the "Eclectic First Reader."

The author is well aware of the important station which books of this grade occupy in the schoolroom, and, in view of this he has expended great labor and pains in its preparation.

Many of the lessons are entirely new. Others have been recomposed, simplified, and divested of objectionable and unintelligible expressions; while some have been abridged, and otherwise modified, both in language and sentiment, that they might be easy of apprehension to that class of readers for which the book is designed.

No one who has not had experience in the preparation of books for the schoolroom, or paid particular attention to this subject, can conceive how utterly unsuitable, for purposes of instruction, is much of the juvenile reading placed before our youth.

If this little volume should meet the wants of teachers, and assist them in the instruction of their pupils, the author will be amply rewarded for his undertaking.

The system of Spelling Lessons, adopted in the First Reader, has been continued in the Second; and it is presumed, that those teachers who have tested its utility, have had satisfactory demonstration of the beneficial effects of blending Spelling Lessons with Reading.

CONTENTS.

SUGGESTIONS TO TEACHERS.

The first object of the intelligent teacher, is to awaken the attention of his pupils. This can be accomplished in no other way so well as by asking him questions. The questions found at the end of the Lessons, are intended merely as hints to the teacher, of the way in which he may exercise the mind of the learner on every subject that is brought before him.

In using this book, the teacher is requested to try the *conversational* mode of communicating instruction, and of training the mind. Let him use the questions, furnished in the book, as the basis of this method; but let him, by no means, confine himself to these alone.

Nothing can be more fatiguing to the teacher, nor irksome to the pupil, than a recitation conducted on the plan of "verbatim answers, to questions not always the most pertinent nor perspicuous." And even if the questions found in the book *were* the *most* pertinent, still it would be but little more than an exercise of memory, to the neglect of the other faculties, to *confine* the examinations exclusively to these.

Let teachers strive to fix the attention of their pupils upon *everything* found on the page assigned for recitation. Let them call for answers and explanations; and let them never *refuse* or *delay* to give such answers, and to make such explanations, as shall not only render intelligible, but make interesting, every picture, every story, and every *Spelling Lesson* in the book.

Accuracy is too little valued in school instruction. Nothing is of much value which is not *accurately* acquired: and yet that accuracy, which consists in an adherence to the precise language, as well as ideas, of the Lesson, is of but little value.

Let the child be encouraged to tell over the story, which he has just read, in language of his own. Let his faults be pointed out to him, with such simplicity, and clearness of illustration as shall make him sensible of what is meant,—and with such kindness, as shall secure his gratitude for the corrections made: and those teachers who have not before tried the experiment, will, it is believed, be surprised at its results.

In conclusion,—let teachers be assured, that any method of teaching, even the alphabet, which does not exercise their own minds, so as to give a pleasurable excitement of thought, will not be successful in securing the object which every instructor ought mainly to propose to himself, namely, the interest and improvement of his pupils.

ECLECTIC SECOND READER.

LESSON I.
The Little Readers.

1. Frank, what a fine thing it is to read. A little while ago, you know, you could only read little words, and you had to spell them—c-a-t, cat; d-o-g, dog.

2. You were a long time getting through with the "First Reader," but now you can read quite well.

3. Do you know why you are better than Puss? Puss can play as well as you and can run as fast as you, and faster too. She can climb trees better, and she can catch mice, which you cannot do.

4. Can she talk? No. Can she read? No. Then that is a reason why you are better than Puss—because you can talk and read.

5. Can you teach Tray to read? Take a pin, and point to the words. No, he will not learn.

6. I never saw a dog nor a cat learn to read. Little boys can learn, and they must strive to learn their lessons well.

Questions.—1. Is it a fine thing to read? 2. Could you always read? 3. What were you a long time getting through? 4. Why are you better than Puss?

what	Puss	point	spell
thing	play	words	catch
while	trees	learn	task
know	mice	strive	well
should	which	could	climb
forced	better	faster	because
cannot	reason	never	little
lessons	reader	only	getting

LESSON II.

Time to Get Up.

1. James, it is now morning. The sun is just peeping over the hills in the east. Get up, my boy, for the sun has just risen!

2. I hope you have said your prayers, and thanked your Father in Heaven for all His goodness. I hope you have thanked Him for your good health, and the blessing of a home, for kind parents, for tender friends, for pleasant books, and all your other enjoyments.

3. Never forget, before you leave your room, to thank God for His kindness. He is indeed kinder to us than an earthly parent.

4. Let us now go out of doors. How beautifully the sun shines upon the hills! How glorious a thing is the sun. How much like that Being who dwells in the Heavens, sending down His mercies upon mankind, as the sun sheds its light and its warmth upon the world!

Questions.—1. When does the sun rise? 2. Where does it rise? 3. Did you say your prayers this morning? 4. Who is kinder to you than a parent? 5. Where does He dwell?

kind	friends	books	leave
men	shines	thank	doors
dwells	down	sheds	light
warmth	world	your	much
thine	health	east	James
morning	keeping	risen	glorious
father	heaven	thanked	enjoyment
blessings	tender	pleasant	beautiful
mercies	indeed	kinder	mankind

LESSON III.
The Little Idle Boy.

1. There was a little boy. He was not a big boy, for if he had been a big boy, I suppose he would have been wiser. This was a little boy, not higher than the table, and his papa and mama sent him to school.

2. It was a very fine morning. The sun shone, and the birds sang in the trees.

3. Now this little boy did not love his books very much, for he was a silly little boy. As I told you, he had a great mind to play, instead of going to school.

4. He saw a bee flying about, first upon one flower, and then upon another; so he said, "Pretty bee! Will you come and play with me?"

5. The bee said, "No, I must not be idle, I must go and gather honey."

Questions.—1. What is this story about? 2. Was he a wise boy? 3. Where did his parents send him?   4. Did he love his books? 5. Can little boys become wise if they do not love their books?

much	those	would	trees
saw	great	book	sent
told	mind	must	him
than	first	there	wall
love	said	come	fine
upon	suppose	mama	morning
flower	instead	flying	another
higher	pretty	gather	honey

LESSON IV.
The Idle Boy Reformed.

1. After this the little idle boy met a dog, and he said, "Dog! Will you play with me?" But the dog said, "No, I must not be idle. I am going to catch a hare for my master's dinner. I must make haste and catch it."

2. Then the little boy went by a hayrack, and he saw a bird pulling some hay out of the hayrack, and he said, "Bird! Will you come and play with me?"

3. But the bird said, "No! I must not be idle; I must get some hay to build my nest, and some moss, and some wool." So the bird flew away.

4. Then the little boy saw a horse, and he said, "Horse! Will you play with me?" But the horse said, "No, I must not be idle; I must go and plow, or else there will be no corn to make bread."

5. Then the little boy thought to himself: "What, is no one idle? Then little boys must not be idle." So he

hurried to school, and learned his lesson very well, and the master said he was a very good boy.

––––––––––

Questions.—1. What little boy was this? 2. What did he want the dog to do? 3. Would the dog go with him? 4. Ought he not to have felt ashamed? 5. Can dogs and birds and horses talk?

plow	make	boy	build
there	will	must	thought
what	some	horse	school
haste	idle	bird	very
play	good	well	catch
learned	growing	master	dinner
little	pulling	neither	nobody
lesson	himself		

LESSON V.
The New Kite.

1. A few days ago, as James Pratt was on his road to a field near home, he met John Reed with a new kite in his hand.

2. "You have a nice kite there," said James, "what did you give for it?"

3. "I gave just ten cents for it," said John. "Do you think it cheap, or expensive?"

4. "I think," said James, "it was very cheap. I wish I could get one at the same price—but where is your cord?"

5. John said he had it in his hand. He held it up, and told James that it was long, and strong.

6. "Now," said James, "let's go to the top of the hill, and make it fly." John liked the sport, and was glad to have James go with him.

7. When they got to the top of the hill, they soon set off the kite. It rose high, but the wind was too strong, so it soon fell to the ground.

8. On its way down, it met with a dead branch of an old tree, which tore a large hole in it. They knew how to mend it when they got home.

Questions.—1. What is this story about? 2. Where was James going? 3. What is a kite made of? 4. Can you make a kite? 5. Can you tell me what Dr. Benjamin Franklin did with a kite? 6. Where did John get his kite?

was	few	field	James
high	which	near	John
kite	down	home	nice
just	since	could	there
with	mend	knew	wind
said	when	gave	hand
own	they	make	long
off	what	wish	pray
one	cents	such	cord
old	cheap	same	soon
tree	dear	price	ground
sport	branch	large	strong

LESSON VI.
The Kite Lost.

1. The next day they went to the same spot, with the kite as good as new, and with a hope to have good sport, as the wind was not too high.

2 When they set it off, its fine long tail hung with great grace in the air. It soon was so high, that it took the whole length of the cord.

3. James had hold of the cord, and he gave it a kind of jerk, and broke it. So the kite flew away like a great bird.

4. "Oh, what have you *done*?" said John. James told the truth, and said he was very sorry.

5. "Well," said John, "we may as well go home now; we can do nothing more. If we run to catch it, we shall run in vain. If we sit down and cry, that will not bring back the kite. If I were to beat you, it would be wrong, and would do me no good."

6 What a good boy John Reed is! I hope that he will soon have a new kite, and that all the boys who know him, will be as kind to him as he was to James Pratt."

Questions.—1. What boys were these? 2. What did they have?   3. What did James do to it?   4. How did John feel about it? 5. Was this better than to get angry?   6. Is it ever right to be angry?

beat	next	sport	grace
soon	good	great	hang
wrong	new	wind	hung
John	give	flew	catch
James	jerk	flown	shall
Reed	break	bird	vain
Pratt	broke	truth	bring
whole	length	hold	back

LESSON VII.

The Cat and Ball.

1. One fine summer day, Mr. Smith took his children with him to a toy-shop, and bought them many new playthings.

2. Emma chose a neat willow basket. John was most pleased with a cup and ball, and Alfred chose something that we shall mention in another story.

3. When they came home, they sat down under an apple tree in the garden, and began to play with the cup and

ball. The cat was sitting behind a rose-bush, watching the little birds on the trees.

4. As soon as Puss saw them trying to catch the ball in the cup, she thought that she could join in the sport. So she left watching the birds, and crept slyly along, to watch the ball and the string.

5. Emma was tossing the ball, and trying to catch it oftener than her brothers had done. She did not see the cat, till Puss leaped into her lap, and seized the string and ball.

6. It made them all laugh very heartily, to see her sit and watch the ball, as she would a mouse or a bird, and then leap after it into Emma's lap.

7. Puss tried once to carry it away, but they all agreed that this was wrong. They showed her that she might have her share of the sport, but must not spoil theirs.

8. I have seen some boys and girls, who were like this selfish cat. They could never see any playthings, without wanting them. When they were playing with others, they wanted

to have all the play, and let the others look on, and praise them.

———————————

Questions.—1. Where did Mr. Smith take his children? 2. What did Emma choose? 3. What did they do when they got home? 4. What did Puss do? 5. Whom was she like? 6. Does selfishness destroy happiness? 7. Are children often selfish when they do not think of it?

Smith	thought	catch	leap
laugh	took	most	soon
bought	them	ball	join
down	trees	might	some
praise	sport	boys	when
they	saw	thing	girls
selfish	apple	Alfred	mention
summer	little	Emma	playthings
children	willow	seized	others
behind	watching	jumping	wanted
heartily	began	trying	without

LESSON VIII.
About the Beaver.

1. The beaver is about two feet long, and one foot high. It is a light brown color, and its fur is very fine.

2. Few animals show a greater degree of wisdom than the beaver.

3. When summer comes, a great many beavers get together, and build their houses. They have rooms to their houses.

4. When a beaver has no one to help him, he cannot do much.

5. Sometimes two hundred beavers live together. Can you count to two hundred?

6. The beaver has a tail as flat as a shingle. He uses his tail for a trowel. Did you ever see a mason use his trowel? Will you show me how he used it?

7. The beavers cut down very large trees with their teeth. They make their houses of wood and mortar.

8. A beaver can live in the water, and he can live out of the water. Beavers like to build their houses close to a river or pond. Their fur is used to make hats.

Questions.—1. What is this story about? 2. Is the beaver an ingenious animal? 3. What does he build? 4. Could you build a house? 5. Do beavers like to live together? 6. Of what use is their fur?

thick	walls	large	trees
make	takes	house	much
beaver	wisdom	pretty	summer
color	cannot	count	hundred
greater	trowel	mason	mortar
build			

LESSON IX.

About the Moon.

1. The moon shines at night. Sometimes it looks like a bow that is bent, and sometimes it appears round. When it appears quite round, it is called the full moon.

2. The moon does not give as much light as the sun. It gives a mild and beautiful light, and often renders the night very pleasant, when otherwise it would be dark and gloomy.

3. In summer, it is delightful to walk by moonlight. The air then is soft and refreshing, the winds play gently among the trees and shrubs. The little streams, as they flow on, catch the beams of the moon and seem to toss them about while children play with little toys.

4. All around is still, so that you can hear the slightest noise. The quivering of the leaves seems like the whispers of people nearby. The sighing of the winds in the grass appears like the voice of someone flying unseen through the air.

5. The notes of a flute at a distance come to the ear with wonderful clearness. The rumbling of a wagon far off, sounds near at hand, and the barking of the watch dog on the distant hill seems as if it were at the next house.

6. How beautiful are the trees in the moonlight. Everything that is not pleasing is hidden by the darkness, and only that which is lovely comes to view. Thus, all that we see, all that we hear, all that we feel, brings us pleasure in the serene moonlight.

7. Oh! How the sense of smell is refreshed with the fragrance of flowers and the sweet scent of the newmown hay at this delightful season!

8. I hope my little readers will think of these things, and go forth, and see

if they are not true. When they find them to be so, I hope they will look up and give thanks unto Him who has sent them the pleasure of the summer moonlight evening.

———

Questions.—1. When does the moon shine?   2. Can you tell me why it does not shine in the day time?   3. How far is the moon from the earth?   4. Do you think people live upon the moon?   5. When is it pleasant to walk out?   6. When is there a softness given to music?

gently	unseen	summer	moonlight
renders	sighing	pleasure	wonderful
smell	appears	evening	delightful
sense	readers	whispers	thanksgiving
often	distant	beautiful	sometimes
flying	secure	rumbling	slighest

LESSON X.
A Merry Sleigh Ride.

1. "We are to have a sleigh ride today," said William, "and I mean to drive."

2. "You cannot drive," said Andrew, "you are too small. You are only four years old."

3. "Yes, yes, I can drive," said William, "I am big enough, and I can make old Dobbin gallop. Come Susan, Patty, and Andrew. The sleigh is ready. Let us all get in."

4. So, they all jumped in, and began to ride away very happily.

5. Then William said to the driver "Now, Moses, let me drive a little." Moses told him that he would turn them all over, but William begged to drive, and Moses gave him the reins.

6. Then he felt very brave, and called out "Get up, get up, hie! Away,

old Dobbin." He cracked his whip, and shook the reins, and the horse galloped away at a great rate.

7. "See how we go," said William; "now we shall have a grand ride." And so they had, till they came to a short turn in the road, and the sleigh overturned.

Questions.—1. What is this story about?   2. What did William want to do? 3. What did he do?   4. What is a sleigh?

sleigh	years	reins	grand
brave	road	come	they
William	called	tumbled	upset
Andrew	servant	enough	began
Dobbin	galloped	cracked	away
where	arrive		

LESSON XI.
The love of Brothers and Sisters.

1. Sweet is the song of birds, when the dark days of winter are over and gone. The trees lift up their green heads in the bright light of spring.

2. Sweet is the sport of the lambkins, while their mothers lie down to sleep by the little stream that flows in the cool shade.

3. Sweet is the hum of bees when the work of the day is done, and they fold their wings to rest in the full hive.

4. Sweet is the shout of joy which is heard at the farm when the last load of corn is brought home, and the tables are spread for the harvest feast.

5. But far more sweet than any of these is the love of brothers and sisters for each other. It takes away many a sad tear from grief. And, oh, with what joy is it seen by the fond father and mother.

6. They press their good and kind children to their breasts, and pray God to bless them. And God doth and will bless them. The good find favor in His sight, and His tender mercy is upon them forever.

7. My little reader, have you brothers and sisters? Then love them with all your heart. Do all you can for them. Help them when in need; and do

not wait to be asked. Add to their mirth. Share their grief. Do not make them angry. Use no cross words.

8. Touch not what is not your own. Speak the truth at all times. Do no wrong, but do unto them as you would have them do unto you. So shall you make the hearts of your parents rejoice. So shall you have the blessing of the great God who made you.

Questions.—1. What is this lesson about?   2. What is said of the song of birds, and the sport of lambkins?   3. What is sweeter far than these?   4. What should children do for each other?   5. If children love and help each other, will they not be loved by those who see them?

green	blithe	winter	reader
share	laugh	harvest	mercy
grief	sight	tables	other
hearts	cross	father	away
little	many	lesson	asked
tender	children	blessing	rejoice
streamlet	lambkins	brothers	

LESSON XII.
The Greedy Girl.

1. Laura is a greedy girl. Indeed she is quite a glutton. Do little girls know what a glutton is? Any one is a glutton who eats too much food, because it tastes well.

2. Laura's mother allows her to have as many nice things as are good for her, but sometimes, when she is not watching, Laura eats too much, and then she is sick.

3. I don't know what makes her such a silly girl. Her kitten never eats more than it wants. It leaves the nice bones of meat in the plate, and lies down to sleep, when it has eaten enough.

4. Her canary birds are not so silly. If she fills their cage with seed, they will only eat what they want, and leave the rest till tomorrow.

5. The busy bee is wiser than Laura. It flies about among the flowers, and might eat out of the honey-cups all day, if it pleased. It only eats enough to keep it alive and well, and carries the rest home to her hive.

6. The pretty squirrel eats a half a dozen acorns, and frisks about as if he had dined at the king's table. Did you never see a squirrel with a nut in its paws? How bright and lively he looks. How he runs along the stone wall, as quick as if a boy had shot him from his popgun!

7. If he lived in a house made of acorns, he would never need to have a doctor come to see him. He would not eat a single acorn more than he wanted, just because they tasted good.

8. I do not love little girls that eat too much. I do not think they will have such rosy cheeks, or such bright eyes, or such sweet lips, or such happy tempers, as those who eat less. Do you, my little readers?

———————

Questions.—1. Who is a greedy girl? 2. What is it to be greedy? 3. What is wiser than a greedy girl? 4. Do brute animals often reprove little children for their bad habits? 5. When we find we are doing wrong what ought we to do?

stone	fills	cheeks	much
house	flies	girls	such
silly	busy	lived	about
only	wiser	doctor	wanted
bones	half	tastes	from
honey	lively	popgun	squirrel
acorn	never	happy	dozen
kitten	body	Laura	tempers

LESSON XIII.

Time to go to Bed.

1. It is evening. The sun is setting behind the mountains, and the shadows begin to darken the forests.

2. The birds have ceased to sing, except as lonely robin or a thrush, that sits upon the top of a tree, and sings a plaintive hymn.

3. The farmer has left the field and is going to his happy home. The bee is silent in the hive. The buzzing insects are still, and the fowls, who, a little while ago, were filling the air with their notes, are heard no more.

4. All around us seem to seek repose, and the very hills and valleys appear

to be sinking into gentle sleep. We too must now retire to our pillows.

5. Before we close our eyes, let us lift up our hearts in gratitude to that Great Being who never sleeps, but watches over us, as the shepherd watches over his flock.

6. Let us ask His forgiveness for our faults and His aid to avoid every sin. Let us seek His friendship, and ask Him to assist us to be kind and amiable to our brothers and sisters, and companions—to be gentle to every living thing, to obey and love our parents, to respect the aged, and to be kind to the sick and to the poor.

7. Above all, let us ask God to fill our hearts with love for Him, to inspire us with a love of everything that is good, and to refrain from everything that is evil. Let us ask Him to make us love to tell the truth, and to be ashamed to tell a lie.

8. Let us ask Him to watch over us in our sleep when darkness is around us, and none but He is awake to keep us from evil.

Questions.—1. What part of the day is it when the birds cease to sing? 2. Who is it that keeps the birds and the bees alive when they are asleep? 3. Who takes care of you when you are asleep? 4. Ought you to love Him, and serve Him while you are awake?

watch	evening	appear	refrain
friend	shadows	inspire	forest
robin	ceased	confidence	lonely
keep	amiable	gratitude	repose
safely	setting	ashamed	sinking
resign	darken	mountains	darkness
valleys	except	whatever	protector
before	filling	ourselves	daughters

LESSON XIV.

About the Stars.

1. What child is there, that has never looked up with wonder at the stars!

2. I once knew a little boy, who, after looking at them for a long time, went

to his mother and said, "Mother, these bright things in the sky, you call stars, but I think that is not the right name for them?"

3. "Well my child," said his mother, "what do you think they are?"

4. "Why, I think they are God's candles," said the boy. This idea is at once natural and beautiful. They indeed seem like lamps set in the glorious Hall of the Creator, to show forth its grandeur, and call upon the universe to worship Him who sitteth upon the throne, for ever and ever.

5. Whatever the stars may *seem* to be, we have reason to suppose that they are worlds, or suns, much larger than the moon, or even than this earth.

6. How wonderful then are these shining orbs, and how great must He be, who in wisdom and goodness has made them all!

7. We must often think of the Lord, who is so great and good. We must love Him with all our hearts, and try to do His will.

8. Let us look up to Him with love and praise, and indulge in the hope, that when we leave this earth, He will take us to heaven. There we may study the stars, and learn all the glorious things that He has done.

Questions.—1. What is this lesson about?   2. What did a little boy once say to his mother?   3. Was this a beautiful idea?   4. What do you suppose the stars are?   5. Who made the stars?   6. Do you suppose they stand still?

praise	lamps	wonder	adoration
bright	hearts	natural	glorious
there	child	grandeur	heaven
show	long	shining	indulge
stars	heaven	mother	beings
where	looked	worship	whatever
right	candles	sitteth	suppose
what	indeed	countless	living
forth	wisdom	multitudes	goodness
things	sitteth	wonderful	reason

LESSON XV.

The Sailor Boys.

1. Charles had a wish to be a little sailor boy, and go out upon the deep waters. But his mama would not let him. One day Charles bought a little boat, with a mast, sails, a flag, and ropes. As soon as he brought it home, he placed it carefully in the closet among the other playthings.

2. A few days after, he saw a large tub of water, standing near the garden gate, and he thought it would be a nice

place to sail his boat. He soon got it, and sat down with his brother and sister, to make it sail in the tub.

3. Emma went and brought a piece of thread, which she tied to the vessel, so that they could make it go wherever they pleased. William then made a little boat of paper, and they sailed finely together.

4. The children thought this very good sport. John said he meant to catch some little fishes, and let them live in the tub, and then it would be a fine pond.

5. Just at this moment Polly came along, and called out, "Away, away, are you not ashamed of yourselves, to be stirring the water, and making it dirty."

6. "O never mind that," said Charles; "Only see how fine my boat sails." "I cannot help that," said Polly, "I have taken pains to get this clean water to wash the linen, and it shall not be spoiled for all the boats in Cincinnati."

7. So they were obliged to take away the boats, and find a safer pond for them. They did it cheerfully when they saw that this was not a proper place for them.

8. When Polly saw how kind they were about it, she loved them, and said she would make a very pretty play for them when she had done her work.

Questions.—1. What did Charles wish to be? 2. What is a sailor? 3. What did Charles buy? 4. Of what use are ships? 5. Do ships ever sink when they are at sea? 6. What then becomes of the sailors?

thread	after	beautiful	brother
brought	placed	water	vessel
among	careful	standing	wherever
tied	pretty	carefully	Cincinnati
fishes	paper	moment	making
linen	sailed	together	dirty
safer	finely	ashamed	obliged
closet	away	yourselves	stirring

LESSON XVI.

The Kind Little Girl.

1. Ann was a child five years old. She was good and kind to all. The girls who went to school with her were fond of her. The beasts and birds around the house would come when they heard her voice.

2. All the fowls in the yard would run to her as soon as they saw her. She was glad when she got permission to feed them.

3. One day when she came from school she met her mother, who gave her a cake. It was a fine day so she went to the field at the back of the house to eat it.

4. She had just sat down by the fence, when a poor thin dog came to look at her. She gave him a small bit of her cake, and saw him eat it and wag his tail. Then an old man came out of a poor hut to call the dog, and Ann saw that he too was thin, pale, and sick.

5. She gave him a large piece of her cake, and he said, "Thank you, good

child!" and ate it, and told her that it did him good. The old man and his dog then went back to the hut, and Ann ate the small bit of cake that was left. She felt much better than if she had eaten the whole cake.

6. She was fond of cakes. I am not sure, if the old man and his dog had been fat and strong, that she would have thought of giving them a bit. They did not ask for it, but she saw that they were in great need, which reminded her to share with them.

7. It was not long before Ann had another cake. As soon as she received it, she went to look for the old man and his dog, but could not find them. She met a boy who told her that they had grown fat and well, and had gone to their own home, far away.

Questions.—1. How old was Ann? 2. Who were fond of her? 3. Will children always be loved, if they are good? 4. What did Anna's mother give her one day? 5. What did Ann do with it? 6. Was this right? 7. Ought we to be kind to the poor, and supply their wants?

school	fence	man	fond
beasts	field	small	been
would	just	piece	them
heard	poor	went	thought
they	gone	own	long
around	another	whole	cakes
mother	eaten	grown	fond
giving	better	great	

LESSON XVII.
Edward and the Cat.

1. "Mother," said little Edward, one day, "our cat ought to be killed." His mother wondered to hear her little boy talk and look so ill-natured. She said, "Why Edward, what has poor Puss done?"

2. "Why, mother, I give her milk and meat, and make a nice bed for her and all, and yet she won't mind a word I say. When I try to drive her out of the room, she won't go unless she pleases, and when I try to push her, she growls, and sometimes she will not let me even stroke her back."

3. "Should she be killed, because she does not love nor mind *you*?" said his mother. "Yes ma'am, since I am so kind to her." "Stop, my son, and think a little—poor Puss is a dumb animal, she does not know right from wrong. Cannot you forgive her?"

4. Edward looked a little ashamed at being so unmerciful, but he said rather pettishly, "I wish we had a kind cat. I don't like cross ones."

5. His mother did not say anything more at that time, but she remembered how Edward wanted to have the poor cat put to death. She was sorry to think he showed so little mercy, and that he thought so much of his own kindness.

6. The Lord said, "Blessed are the merciful, for they shall obtain mercy," and "Blessed are the meek, for they shall inherit the earth." Little Edward lacked kindness for the cat, and he lacked meekness, but he could not bear that even poor Puss should not obey and love him when he was kind.

7. The next day Edward was sitting by the fire shelling corn for his

chickens, and looking very happy, when his mother said, "My son, that is a nice fire, are you warm and comfortable?"

8. "Oh, yes, ma'am." "Are your shoes and clothes warm and good?" "Why yes, mother, you know I have very good clothes, and a great coat and all."

9. "Is your bed soft and warm?" "Why, mother, what makes you ask me, you know there are two or three blankets on it, and I almost always sleep warm the whole night without waking."

10. "Never mind why I ask you, yet," said his mother, "only answer me—have you good food and drink?" "Yes ma'am, and often more than I want." "Where do all these good things come from?" "God gives them to me, mother." "Do you then love Him, and mind Him, and try to please Him always?"

11. Edward knew he did not, and so he did not like to speak—he held his head down, and his mother said, "Then,

my son, don't you think you ought to be killed?" The little boy opened his eyes wide, saying, "Mother! *killed!*"

12. "Why," said his mother, "*you* certainly must think so, for you thought the cat ought to be killed, because she did not love you, and mind when you were kind to her?" Edward's face turned red, for he began to see now why his mother had asked all these questions.

Questions.—1. What did Edward say ought to be done with the cat? 2. Why did he wish her to be killed? 3. What kind of feeling did Edward's mother wish him to have? 4. What is it to be merciful? 5. Ought we not to be merciful?

always	never	mother	masters
because	Edward	opened	blessed
turned	ought	blankets	forgive
questions	when	shelling	sitting
obtain	why	mercy	therefore
began	down	cannot	chickens
feeling	earth	remember	killed
happy	good	certainly	merciful
looking	things	meekness	inherit
kindness	clothes	chestnut	

LESSON XVIII.
The Three Happy Children.

1. I once knew two charming little girls, and a smiling boy, who were very happy! They loved each other fondly, and what was the joy of one was the joy of all.

2. I can fancy I see them now, seated all three in the shade, their heads closely meeting as they read the same book, or looked at the same pictures. Their parents were very kind to them, and could afford them many fine things, but their chief bliss arose from the love they had for each other.

3. If one was in trouble, the others would unite to help him out of it, and if one was sick, he was sure at least of two good nurses. Had one a cake or an orange, it was worth nothing till shared with the other two.

4. No murmurs were heard, where they lived. There was much good feeling among them. If one played a tune on the piano, the other two would stand by, and sing to the merry music.

5. If a letter was to be written, one would write and the others help to spell the words, and think what was best to say. If a lesson was to be learned, there was such hearing, prompting, and helping, that the lesson was soon learned by all.

6. With the early dawn, they sprang from their beds to meet each other, and not till the firefly was shining on the dark turf did they part, with many tender "Good-nights."

7. Always at peace with each other, they were at peace with all the world. No harsh words passed their lips, no

frowns darkened their brows, no selfish feelings disturbed their happiness.

8. They were not handsome, but people thought them lovely, because their looks were so gentle, their manners so mild, and frank, and pleasing.

9. By their conduct, these three good children secured their own joy. They gained the love and esteem of all around them.

———————————◆———————————

Questions.—1. What is this story about? 2. How many children were there? 3. Did they love each other? 4. How did they show their benevolence? 5. Do you not think that such behavior must have endeared them to one another? 6. Who has commanded little children to love one another? 7. If we let love run through all our actions shall we not avoid a great deal of trouble in life?

knew	gentle	pleased	around
chief	played	trouble	people
could	mercy	shining	esteem
would	music	conduct	darkened
thought	others	because	prompting
gained	chosen	passed	laughing
clever	letter	caused	smiling

LESSON XIX.
The Boys who did Mischief for Fun.

1. I will tell you another story. William and Edward were two clever little boys, and not at all ill-natured. They were very fond of sport, and they did not care whether people were hurt or not, provided they could have a laugh.

2. One fine summer's day, when they had said their lessons, they took a walk through the long grass in the meadows. William began to blow the dandelions, and the feathered seeds flew in the wind like arrows.

3. But Edward said, "Let us tie the grass. It will be very good sport to tie the long grass over the path, and to see people tumble upon their noses as they run along, and do not suspect any thing of the matter."

4. So they tied it in several places, and then hid themselves to see who would pass. Presently a farmer's boy came running along, and down he tumbled, and lay sprawling on the

ground. He had nothing to do but to get up again, so there was not much harm done this time.

5. Then there came Susan the milk-maid, tripping along with her milk upon her head, and singing like a lark. When her foot struck against the place where the grass was tied, down she came with her pail rattling about her shoulders, and her milk was all spilled upon the ground.

6. Then Edward said, "Poor Susan! I think I should not like to be treated like that, let us untie the grass."—"No, no," said William, "If the milk is spilled, there are some pigs that will lick it up, let us have more fun. I see a man running along as if he were running for a bet. I am sure he will fall upon his nose."

7. And so the man did. William and Edward both laughed, but when the man did not get up again, they began to be frightened, and went to him, and asked him if he were hurt.

8. "Oh, masters," said the man, "some thoughtless boys I do not know

who they are, have tied the grass together over the path, and as I was running with all my might, it threw me down, and I have sprained my ankle so that I shall not be able to walk for a month."

9. "I am very sorry," said Edward; "Do you feel much pain?"—"Oh, yes," said the man, "that I do not mind, but I was going in a great hurry to bring a surgeon to save a man's life."

10 Then Edward and William both turned pale, and said, "Where does the surgeon live? We will go for him, we will run all the way."—"He lives at the next town," said the man, "but it is a mile off, and you cannot run so fast as I should have done, you are only boys."

11. "Where must we tell the surgeon to come to?" said William. "He must come to the white house, at the end of the long chestnut avenue," said the man. "He is a very good gentleman that lives there."

12. "Oh, it is our dear father! It is our dear father!" said the two boys, "Oh, father will die, what must we do?"

13. I do not know whether their papa died or not. I believe he got well again, but I am sure of one thing, that Edward and William never tied the grass to throw people down again as long as they lived.

———————

Questions.—1. What is this story about? 2. Where did William and Edward go one day? 3. What did they do in the field? 4. Was it not very wicked for them to do such things? 5. When we begin to do mischief, can we tell where we shall stop? 6. How did these boys feel when they found what they had done?

grass	people	sprained	gentleman
thing	again	laughed	sprawling
know	never	meadows	presently
threw	clever	chestnut	shoulders
through	surgeon	myself	trudging
there	lived	running	Edward
flew	cruel	whether	William
down	going	harmless	brightened
believe	began	avenue	thoughtless

LESSON XX.

Story about Whales.

1. A whale is a large mammal. There is no beast so large as a whale. They

have been seen of such large sizes, that they look like land as they float on the surface of the sea.

2. They have a large mouth, but a small throat, so that they cannot eat large fish. The tongue is a lump of fat, which yields a great deal of oil, their eyes are small and have lids to them. They have fins and a large tail, which they lash when in a rage or pain. This causes the sea to foam.

3. One blow from the tail of a whale will sink a boat in the sea. The tail is used when it swims, and its fins help it to turn. When the whale is in fear for her young, she takes them on her back and puts them up on her fins, so that they cannot fall. They take great care of their young. They are fond of their young.

4. The head of the whale is about one third of its length, and when its mouth is open, it is capable of holding a ship's jolly boat filled with men.

5. You would think that a whale can have no fears, because it is so large and strong. There is a fish called the sword

fish, which the whale dreads, and which he tries to shun in all ways, or to strike with his tail.

6. In vain it tries. The sword fish is so swift and strong, that it jumps out of the sea into the air, then darts down on the whale, and wounds it with its sharp sword-like snout or nose. The sea becomes red with the blood of the whale.

———————

Questions.—1. What is this story about? 2. What is a whale? 3. When the whale is frightened, what does it do with its young? 4. What fish is that which troubles the whale? 5. In what way does it make its attack? 6. Is the whale the largest animal that lives?

whale	throat	great	lash
they	which	takes	swift
mouth	there	round	strong
lump	seen	swims	tries
large	tongue	would	does
have	yields	dread	bounds
small	bags	strike	dangerous
wounds	large	quick	catching
fish	blow	think	harpoon
been	swift	sword	sometimes

LESSON XXI.

Stories about Whale Catching.

1. Men kill whales with a sharp iron spear, or harpoon. This they throw at the whale with great force. When the whale is struck, it dives down into the sea, out of sight, but it soon comes up to the top for air.

2. The men are on the watch for this. As soon as they see it rise, they strike it with their harpoons till it dies.

3. The men tie ropes to their harpoons, which are made fast to the boat, so that they may not be lost when they miss their aim. When the whale is

dead, it is cut, and those parts which yield the oil are put into casks.

4. Directly under the skin lies the blubber or fat. This surrounds the whole body, and is from ten to twenty inches thick. In its fresh state it has no unpleasant smell. The oil which we burn in our lamps is made from this.

5. In the picture you see the whale has thrown the boat into the air, and the men have been knocked in every direction.

6. Catching whales is very dangerous. Sometimes the whales get angry and plunge about with great fury.

7. A whale, with one of its young, was once left by the tide close to the shore. The sea was not deep enough for them to get out again. The men who saw them, took their harpoons and got into their boats to go and kill them, for they were a rich prize.

8. The whales were hurt, but the old one was strong, and with one bold push got clear of her foes, and swam out to the deep sea.

9. She had not been there long, when she found her poor young one was not with her. She swam back into the midst of her foes to seek it. They both had the good fate to be taken back by the flow of the tide, to their safe and wide home in the deep sea.

Questions.—1. What is used to kill whales? 2. When they are killed, what do they do with them?   3. What is taken from the whale that is of service to us?   4. What is said about the young whale and its mother?   5. Why is it dangerous to engage in catching whales?

vast	once	want	knocked
dead	took	made	found
deep	strong	spear	dangerous
prize	miss	struck	picture
minds	close	sight	taken
casks	boats	soon	good
could	push	there	very
much	shore	catching	about
when	quite	angry	lamps

LESSON XXII.

The Truant.

1. Who is he that sleeps till a late hour, and when he wakes, yawns and wishes for the return of night, that he may fold his arms, and sleep again?

2. He is the idle and worthless truant. He comes forth clothed in the garments of slovenliness. In his step is the heaviness of stupid sloth. The scars of strife are on his swollen cheeks.

3. The rage of malice flashes from his eyes. His uncombed hair, all matted, stands erect. On his lips are the words of deceit and falsehood.

4. Ignorance is a cap of disgrace to his head, and vice and impiety dwell in his heart.

5. Behold him as he now skulks along yonder lane. How slyly he walks. He stops to look into every bush, that he sees on his right hand and on his left.

6. He knows that he is not in the way that leads to the object which it is his duty to seek, yet he scorns to turn away from it.

7. His eye looks around for a companion in crime. His ear eagerly listens for the whistled signal.

8. As the voice of the charmer is to the adder, that is too deaf to be charmed, so is the voice of instruction to him that is too vicious to be taught. He creeps into the thick woods, lest he should be seen and sent back to school.

9. The fear of punishment is in his breast, for he had neglected every duty. Learning is his abhorrence, and he loathes those who would teach him. He loathes the knowledge which they would impart to him.

10. He looks upon them as foes, and he flies to folly "as a bird hasteth to the snare, and knoweth not that it is for his life."

11. Wretched are the parents of such a son!—Grief and shame are theirs. His name shall be stamped with the mark of infamy when their poor broken hearts shall molder in the grave!

Questions.—1. What is this lesson about? 2. What is a truant? 3. What is in his breast? 4. How does he feel toward those who could teach him? 5. What effect does such conduct have upon parents? 6. Should you not fear to bring shame and grief upon your parents?

sleeps	taught	stamped	impiety
yawns	adder	hasteth	slovenliness
voice	behold	ignorance	knowledge
creeps	signal	abhorrence	instruction
loathes	listens	companion	neglected
skulks	learning	eagerly	falsehood
wakes	broken	uncombed	garments

LESSON XXIII.

The Good Boy whose parents are poor.

1. The good boy whose parents are poor, rises very early in the morning. All day long he does as much as he can, to help his father and mother.

2. When he goes to school, he walks quickly, and does not lose time on the road. "My parents," says he "are very good to save some of their money in order that I may learn to read and write. They cannot give much, nor can they spare me long, therefore, I must learn as fast as I can. If anybody has time to lose, I am sure I have not.

3. "I should be very sorry when I am a man not to know how to read well in the Bible, and other good books. When I leave my parents, not to be able to read their letters, and to write them word where I am, and how I am doing.

4. "I must also learn accounts, for when I grow up I shall have many things to check, about my work, and what I buy. I shall perhaps have bills to make out, as my father has, and perhaps I shall be employed in a store."

5. When he has finished his lessons, he does not stay to play, but runs home. He wants to see his father and mother, and to help them.

6. He often sees naughty boys in the streets who fight, and steal, and do many bad things. He hears them swear, and call names, and tell lies, but he does not like to be with them, for fear they should make him as bad as they, lest anyone who sees him with them, should think that he too is naughty.

7. When he is at home, he is very industrious. He takes care of the little

children, weeds his father's garden, hoes, rakes it, and sows seed in it.

8. Sometimes he goes with his father to work, then he is very glad. Although he is a little fellow, he works very hard, almost like a man.

9. When he comes home to dinner, he says, "How hungry I am! How good this bread is, and this bacon! Indeed, I think everything we have is very good. I am glad I can work. I hope that I shall soon be able to earn all my clothes, and my food too."

10. When he sees little boys and girls riding on pretty horses, or in coaches, or walking with ladies and gentlemen, and having on very fine clothes, he does not envy them, nor wish to be like them.

11. He says, "I have often been told, and I have read, that it is God who makes some poor, and others rich— that the rich have many troubles which we know nothing about and that the poor, if they are but good, may be very happy. Indeed, I think that when I am good, nobody can be happier than I am.

Questions.—1. What is this lesson about?   2. What feelings did he have toward his parents?   3. What did he do when he had finished his lessons?   4. What does he do when he is at home?   5. Should all little boys and girls be industrious, and try to help their parents?   6. If children are poor should they complain at their lot?   7. Is it not better to be industrious and have a good name, than to possess many riches?

school	early	rises	reckon
good	father	quickly	every
know	naughty	mother	happier
streets	nothing	garden	hungry
takes	walking	therefore	employed
think	lessons	accounts	industrious
coaches	morning	children	sometimes
having	money	indeed	nobody
troubles	letters	walking	finished
fellow	perhaps	ladies	

LESSON XXIV.
The Diligent Scholar.

1. Who is he that leaves his bed, eager to resume his studies, as soon as the soaring lark sees the first ray of sunshine?

2. He is the diligent scholar. He comes forth clothed in the garments of neatness. In his step is the lightness of active industry.

3. The glow of health is on his rosy cheeks. The light of gladness sparkles in his eyes. His graceful locks fall lightly round his neck.

4. On his lips are the words of candor and truth. Knowledge is an ornament of grace to his head. Virtue and piety dwell in his heart.

5. Look at him as he comes across the green, with his satchel of books at his back!

6. How briskly he walks! He stops not to consider whether he shall take the right hand path or the left.

7. He knows which is the nearest way to the object, which it is his duty to seek. He scorns to turn away from it. His eye does not regard the crowd of idle boys. His ear does not listen to their noisy games.

8. As the North Star is to the sailor when he crosses the ocean, so is the

distant schoolhouse to him when he crosses the green.

9. He quickens his footsteps lest he should be a minute late. There is no fear of punishment in his breast, for he has neglected no duty.

10. Learning is his delight. He loves those who teach him as he loves the knowledge which he gains from them. He looks upon them as fathers, from whom he receives that instruction, which has been wisely called the "life of the soul."

11. Happy are the parents of such a son! Gladness and triumph are theirs. His name shall be crowned with honor by the virtuous and the good, when the pious counsels of his father and mother are heard no more, and their heads are laid in the silent grave.

———————

Questions.—1. What is this lesson about? 2. What is said of the diligent scholar? 3. What is his delight? 4. How does he feel towards his teacher? 5. Should not all children love those who are so kind as to teach them?   6. What are the feelings of parents when their children are obedient, and learn their lessons well?

leaves	quicken	footsteps	punishment
hearth	learning	crowned	knowledge
knows	nearest	whether	neglected
counsels	distant	candor	ornament
parents	feeling	diligent	industry
triumph	graceful	graceful	instruction
perhaps	crosses		

LESSON XXV.
The Oak and other Trees.

1. What a fine spreading oak is this. It serves us for a canopy, and shades us so comfortably from the sun! See what a number of acorns hang upon it; they are excellent food for hogs.

2. Do not think that the stately oak is good for nothing. It supplies the hogs with food and it is of great value to us.

3. How large it is! It is larger around than any man ever was. It has

hundreds of branches, thousands of acorns, and still more leaves. It has great roots which run a long way into the ground and spread all around at the bottom.

4. The roots keep it from being blown down by the violent gusts of wind. It is through the roots that the moisture of the earth nourishes it and keeps it alive.

5. Now, Henry, is it not a very strange thing, that this great tree grew at first from a little acorn? Look, here is a young one, called a sapling. It is so little, Charlotte, you will be able to pull it up yourself. There you see the acorn still sticking upon the root.

6. The oak we sit under is probably a hundred years old. When it is cut down it will be called timber; the sawyers will saw it into pieces to be used in building ships and houses.

7. There are many kinds of timber-trees such as ash, elm, chestnut, walnut, and others. When there are a number of trees growing together, the place is called a wood, or forest.

Questions.—1. What are acorns? 2. What trees do they grow upon? 3. Are acorns good to eat? 4. Do all trees have roots? 5. Of what use are the roots to the trees? 6. Are trees of use to us? 7. Will you mention in what ways?

shades	years	spreading	sawyers
hang	bigger	number	building
food	under	branches	encounter
gusts	Henry	bottom	nourishes
still	forest	moisture	yourself
leaves	canopy	sticking	sapling
keeps	timber	Charlotte	provision

LESSON XXVI.
More about Trees.

1. I have noticed that all kinds of trees grow either from seeds or kernels that are found in their fruit. They may grow from little plants taken from the old roots or slips taken from their branches.

2. All timber trees grow without any trouble for the rain waters them. I forgot to mention the bark, which is this outside part.

3. Oak trees are used by tanners and dyers. The dry branches, which are good for nothing else, make cheerful fires. The trees are very valuable. Poor Henry would miss them for traps, tops, and bats are cut out of them.

4. See how pretty birds sit singing on the branches; how glad they must be, when it rains, to shelter themselves among the leaves. Besides, if a heavy shower were to come now, we should be happy to stand under a tree ourselves, provided it was not a thunderstorm; for in thunderstorms the trees often attract the lightning, which makes it very dangerous to be near them.

Questions.—1. Are there many kinds of trees?   2. What is a wood?   3. What do trees grow from?   4. For what is the bark of some kinds of trees used?   5. Do trees attract the lightning?

would	tanners	mention	abstract
forgot	dyers	thunder	lightning
trouble	waters	pretty	cheerful
timbers	without	amongst	appearance
outside	kernels	shower	provided
walking	little	heavy	recollect

LESSON XXVII.
The Peacock.

1. The peacock is the most beautiful bird in the world. Its colors are so rich and various that no human art can make any thing like them.

2. When the peacock walks in the sunshine, every movement gives a thousand shades of coloring which are beautiful and ever varying. The tail of this splendid bird is the most beautiful part of its body.

3. These fine colors exceed the luster of the finest flowers of the fields and

gardens. Like the flowers, they fade every year, and the feathers drop from their bodies. They are renewed every spring.

4. The length of the peacock, from the tip of the bill to the end of the tail, is about three feet eight inches. Some of its longest feathers are four feet long. This bird appears haughty and proud, and loves to display its fine colors to those who are looking on, like those little boys and girls who are proud of their fine clothes.

5. The peacock perches upon high places and lives upon barley and other kinds of grain. Its beautiful plumage does not appear before it is nearly three years old. When it drops its fine feathers in the time of harvest, it does not like to be seen, but seeks to hide itself in some gloomy place.

6. Though the peacock is very beautiful, it utters a very harsh and disgusting cry of *eko, eko, eko,* with the most hideous noise. It cannot sing a pleasant song, like the mockingbird.

7. It is so wicked that it will scarcely live with any other bird, except the pigeon. It tears and spoils everything it gets. This bird was first brought from a far distant country, from the East Indies, and it lives to the age of twenty-five years.

8. Little boys and girls, be not like the peacock, proud and vain, because of your beauty and your fine clothes. Humility and goodness are always to be preferred to beauty.

Questions.—1. What is the most beautiful bird in the world? 2. How does it appear when it walks in the sunshine? 3. How long is the peacock? 4. Can it sing? 5. Where was it first brought from? 6. Why are some children like a peacock? 7. What is better than beauty?

three	display	thousands	animals
years	account	coloring	perches
noise	extent	preferred	haughty
beauty	scarcely	renewed	varying
always	hideous		

LESSON XXVIII.

Story about King Solomon.

.1 Solomon was a very great king, and a very wise man.

2. He built a temple for the worship of God. It was so large, and so richly adorned with gold, and silver, and precious stones, and all manner of beautiful things. Indeed the sun has never shone on any building which was so fine as this.

3. There was no king, anywhere, in all the world, like Solomon for his riches, and his wisdom.

4. He had a fine throne of ivory on which he sat; it was covered over with the finest gold. All his drinking vessels, and all the vessels which were in his palace, were of pure gold.

5. He reigned in the land of Judea, and every one praised, and loved him very much. And God blessed him in such a manner, that there never was any king so great who lived before him. Those whom God blesses, they are indeed blessed.

6. Every one who went out of the land into their own country, told of the wisdom and of the glory of Solomon. Indeed, they did not know how to speak of anything else.

Questions.—1. Who was a great king? 2. Was he very wise? 3. What did he build? 4. Where did he build it?

build	temple	Solomon	called
things	purpose	wisdom	praised
great	servants	vessels	precious
whom	questions	before	beautiful
known	camels	journey	adorned

LESSON XXIX.
More about King Solomon.

1. There was a land far away, which was called Sheba. A queen was the ruler of it. When she heard of the glory of Solomon, she took a long journey, to see, and to talk with him.

2. She came to Jerusalem, the city in which Solomon lived. She brought a very great train of servants, and of camels, that carried spices, and very much gold, and precious stones.

3. That she might know whether he was as wise as had been said, she asked him a great many hard questions; and he answered them all.

4. She paid particular attention to everything which she saw. She noticed the number of his servants, and the splendor of their garments—and especially the beautiful temple which he had built for the worship of God. Her mind was full of admiration.

5. She said to the king, "It was a true report that I heard in my own land, of thy sayings, and of thy wisdom. I did not believe until I came, and saw things as they really are,—and behold, the half was not told me. Thy wisdom and prosperity, are far above anything which I had heard."

6. "Happy," said she, "are thy subjects! Happy are these thy servants, who stand continually before thee, and who hear thy wisdom."

7. And she praised the great God, for His goodness both to him and to his people. "Blessed," she said, "be the Lord thy God which delighteth in thee,

to set thee on the throne of Israel, because the Lord loved Israel forever; therefore, he made thee king, to do judgment and justice."

8. She made the king a large present of gold, and a very great store of spices, and of precious stones. The king also gave costly gifts to her; then she went back to her own land and people.

9. Wouldn't it be a great thing, to be as fine, and wise, and rich, and glorious as Solomon?

10. Indeed it would. Yet we might have all these fine things, and not be happy. Fine clothes, and fine things, cannot make the mind of anyone happy.

11. Solomon found that this was the case. We must have the favor of God, and love and serve Him, or we shall never gain what we are seeking.

Questions.—1. Who lived a great way off? 2. What did she hear? 3. To what city did she come? 4. What did she ask King Solomon? 5. Could he answer them?

6. How was she pleased with what she saw?
7. What did she say to the attendants?
8. What is it to be blessed of God? 9. How can we secure God's blessing on us?

Sheba	purpose	believe	beautiful
lived	whether	subjects	prosperity
spices	questions	sayings	Solomon
asked	costly	wisdom	Jerusalem
present	garments	particular	judgment
happy	temple	attention	continually
never	worship	answered	admiration
favors	entrance	worship	

LESSON XXX.
Little Francis and the Hour-Glass.

1. Little Francis was a very talkative boy. He never saw a new thing without asking a great many questions. His mother was very patient and very kind. She would always answer his questions, when it was proper to do so.

2. Sometimes she would say, "You are not old enough to understand that, my son. When you are ten years old, you may ask me, and I will tell you."

3. When his mother said this, Francis never teased any more. He

knew she always loved to answer him, when he asked proper questions.

4. The first time Francis saw an hourglass, he was very much amused; but he did not know what it was. His mama told him that "an hourglass was made in the shape of the figure 8. The sand is put in at one end and runs through a small hole in the middle. Enough sand is put in the glass to take just an hour to run through."

5. Francis sat and watched the little stream of sand run through. He was impatient because it would not run faster.

6. "Let me shake it, mama," said he, "it is very lazy, it will never get through!"

7. "Oh, yes it will, my son," said his mother. "The sand moves little by little, but it moves *all the time.* When you look at the hands of the clock, you think they go very slowly. They do—but *they never stop!* That is the way they go around twenty-four times every day.

8. "While you are at play, the sand is running out grain by grain, and the hands of the clock are moving second after second. When night comes, the sand in the hourglass has run through twelve times— and the hands of the clock have moved all around its great face.

9. "This is because they keep at work every minute, and cannot stop to think how much they have to do, and how long it will take them."

10. In the afternoon, his mother wanted Francis to learn a little hymn, but he said, "Mother, I can never learn it; it is very long—see, there are six verses!"

11. His mother said, "If you will study all the time, and never stop to ask me how long it will take to learn it; you will be able to say it very soon."

12. Francis followed his mother's advice. He studied line after line, very busily. Every fifteen minutes he said a verse; and in one hour and a half, he knew it all perfectly.

Questions.—1. Who was a talkative boy? 2. How did his mother treat him? 3. How was Francis pleased when he first saw an hourglass? 4. What is an hourglass? 5. How many times will the sand run through the glass during the day?

figure	without	asking	Francis
second	patient	always	sometimes
answer	proper	never	questions
every	watched	mother	understand
faster	because	busily	perfectly
cannot	moving	minutes	followed
little	wished	running	impatient
fifteen	followed	advice	afternoon

LESSON XXXI.
Hay Making.

1. Have you ever seen hay made?

2. It is a very pleasant sight, to see so many people busy storing the hay, before the time when frost and snow will deprive the cows, and horses, of grass.

3. Cows and horses cannot think enough to provide for themselves; so men take care to provide for them.

4. When the grass has grown very high, men come with scythes and cut it down; this is called mowing. It is hard work to mow.

5. Then come the men with rakes and pitchforks, to scatter the grass thinly over the field, that the sun and air may dry it.

6. In the evening, they rake the hay up in rows, and make it into little heaps called haycocks. This keeps it from being spoiled by rain and dew.

7. When the grass is quite dry, it is called hay. To keep this hay for use, it is made into stacks. It must be quite dry before it is made into stacks, or it will not be good all through the winter.

Questions.—1. Why do not cows and horses provide food for winter?   2. How is hay made?   3. How is it put up for winter?

thinks	called	provide	pitchfork
heaps	mowing	storing	enough
grass	horses	scatter	pleasant
quite	through	busy	spoiled
stacks	grown	people	themselves
night	scythes	thinly	evening

LESSON XXXII.

Story about the Lark and the Farmer.

1. An old lark once had a nest of young ones in a field of corn which was almost ripe. She was rather afraid the reapers would be ready to work before her lovely brood were old enough to fly away.

2. One morning, before she took her flight, to seek for something to feed them, "My dear little creatures," said she, "be sure that in my absence, you take the strictest notice of every word you hear, and do not fail to tell me as soon as I come home."

3. Sometime after she was gone, in came the owner of the field and his son. "Well, George," said he, "this corn, I think, is ripe enough to be cut down; so tomorrow morning, as soon as you can see, ask our friends and neighbors to come and help us. Tell them that we will do as much for them the first time they want us."

4. When the old lark came back to her nest, the young ones began to nestle and chirp about her. They asked to be removed as soon as she could.

5. "Hush!" said she, "hold your silly tongues. If the farmer depends upon his friends, and his neighbors, you may take my word for it that his corn will not be reaped tomorrow." The next morning, therefore, she went out again, and left the same orders as before.

6. The owner of the field came soon after, to wait for those he had sent to, but the sun grew hot and not a single man came to help him. "Why, then," said he to his son, "I'll tell you what, my boy; you see, those friends of ours have forgotten us, you must therefore

run to your uncles and cousins, and tell them that I shall expect them tomorrow, early, to help us to reap."

7. Well, this also the young ones told their mother as soon as she came home, and in a sad fright they were. "Never mind it, children," said the old one; "for if that be all, you may take my word for it, that his relatives will not assist him as he seems willing to believe. But mark," said she, "what you hear the next time, and let me know without fail."

8. The old lark went abroad the next day as before, but the poor farmer found that his relatives were as backward as his neighbors. "Why, then," said he, "since your uncles and cousins so neglect us, get a couple of good sickles and we will reap the corn ourselves, my boy."

9. When the young ones told their mother this, she said, "Now, my little dears, we must indeed be gone; for when a man resolves to do his own work himself, you may then depend upon it being done."

Questions.—1. Who had a nest of young ones?   2. What did she say one morning?   3. Who came to the field after she was gone?   4. What did he say?   5. What did the young birds then wish?   6. Did the old bird think there was much danger?   7. When did she think the corn would be reaped?   8. What may we learn from this story?

think	afraid	morning	therefore
brood	enough	fledged	danger
young	drones	reapers	sickle
little	couple	relatives	tomorrow
absence	himself	indeed	resolves
before	another	ourselves	neighbors

LESSON XXXIII.
Praise to God.

1. Come, let us praise God, for He is exceedingly great; let us bless God, for He is very good.

2. He made all things; the sun to rule the day; the moon to shine by night.

3. He made the great whale, and the elephant; and the little worm that crawls upon the ground.

4. The little birds sing praises to God, when they warble sweetly in the green shade.

5. The brooks and rivers praise God, when they murmur melodiously among the smooth pebbles.

6. I will praise God with my voice; for I may praise Him, though I am but a little child.

7. A few years ago, and I was but a little infant; and my tongue was dumb within my mouth.

8. I did not know the great name of God, for my reason was not come unto me.

9. I can now speak, and my tongue shall praise Him; I can think of all His kindness, and my heart shall love Him.

10. Let Him call me, and I will come unto Him; let Him command, and I will obey Him.

11. When I am older, I will praise Him better; and I will never forget God, so long as I live.

Questions.—1. What is the subject of this lesson? 2. Who made the sun, and moon,

and all things that live upon the earth? 3.
Who is it that has protected you from harm,
and now keeps you alive? 4. Will God listen
to the praises of little children? 5. Should
you not, then, praise God for His goodness
to you? 6. Will God accept our praises if our
conduct is not right?

great	smooth	pebbles	elephant
praise	tongue	infant	melodiously
heart	forget	amongst	exceedingly
dumb	better	warble	sweetly
mouth	never	glory	crawls
think	whale	kindness	reason
great	older	command	murmur

LESSON XXXIV.
The Points of the Compass.

1. One day as Harry and his sister
were sitting under a shady tree, Harry
observed that the shadow of the tree
reached almost around the trunk. He
had seen in the morning when he was
at breakfast, that the shadow of the
tree fell only on one side of it.

2. Harry asked his father the reason
of this. His father took him to the door
of the house, and asked him to look
where the sun was, and he saw that it

was opposite the door, and very high in the sky.

3. "Take notice, Harry," said his father, "where you see the sun now, and observe where you see it this evening, when the sun is setting."

4. Harry said he knew where the sun set—that he could not see it from the hall door, but that he could see it from that end of the house, which was at the right hand of the hall door, as you go out.

5. *Father.* "Did you ever observe where it rises?"

6. *Harry.* "Yes, it rose this morning at the other end of the house."

7. *Father.* "It did so. Now do you know where are the south, and the north, and the east, and the west?"

8. *Harry.* "No, but I believe the side of the sky where the sun rises is called the east.

9. *Father.* "It is so, and the side where it sets is called the west. Now you may always know the south and the north, wherever you are, if you know where the sun either rises or sets.

10. If you know where it rises, stand with your left hand towards that part of the sky, and then the part of the sky before your face will be the south, and that part of the sky behind your back will be the north.

11. In the same manner, if you know where the sun sets, turn your right hand towards that place, and the part of the sky opposite to you will be the south."

———————————

Questions.—1. When is the weather hot? 2. Where was Henry sitting? 3. What did he observe? 4. What did he ask his father? 5. Where does the sun rise? 6. Which was is west? 7. Which way is north?

other	either	north	round
manner	father	east	stand
always	obscure	south	back
setting	believe	west	high
hand	left	could	face
summer	generally	shady	notice
weather	desired	under	ever
behind	opposite	reason	rises
morning	towards	shadow	asked

LESSON XXXV.
Story of Little Mary.

1. Little Mary was a great favorite with her father, who used to give her whatever toys, dolls, and other play-things, she wanted.

2. It was not right, that Mary should not care for anything, but such things as these.

3. One day they were in the garden, and he was reading something with which he was greatly pleased. She asked him how he could be so pleased in reading what seemed to her very dull. She was sure she would never read except when she was forced.

4. Mary ought to have known better than this, after all her father had told her. She had as many pretty books given to her, as would make a little library.

5. Instead of smiling at her, as he usually did, he turned away his head with a frown, and put her hand out of his. He turned from her, and went into another part of the garden.

6. Mary did not expect this. She was not a silly little girl, though a very idle one. She hung her head, and wept very bitterly.

7. She did not dare to look at her father all that evening, and she did not cease crying till she fell asleep.

8. The next morning she studied her lessons with more care than she had ever done. Her instructor was surprised to find the idlest scholar in school become the first of the class.

9. When Mary went home from school, she would have told her father, but she was ashamed to see him. She hunted all the books which had been given her, and which she had allowed to lie scattered about with broken playthings, and doll's clothes. She looked into one or two, and began to think that, after all, books were not such dull things as she had thought.

10. After she had put them all together, and arranged them on a shelf, she looked at them with great pleasure, and thought as much of her library, as her father seemed to think of his.

11. When she had put her books in order, she thought to herself that she had a lot to do before she dare again see her father. She hoped he might be as kind to her as he used to be.

12. She examined every book she had, in order to see what she might read with the most profit. The ones which might best enable her to talk with her father about the objects he had often pointed out to her, or how to ask him questions sensibly, and not like a silly little girl who knew nothing.

13. At last, she made a choice of the Eclectic Second Reader, which she read so diligently. In a few days she knew everything which it contained, and could describe different things about it.

14. She was pleased with the knowledge she had gained. She loved her father more than ever because he gave her the books.

————————

Questions.—1. Who was a great favorite with her father? 2. What did he give Mary? 3. Was Mary pleased while her father was reading? 4. Ought she then to

have been silent?   5. How did her father
rebuke her?   6. Was Mary a better girl after
this?   7. What did she do with her little
books?   8. Was this better than to have
scattered them about the house?

down	would	sudden	idle
hand	rebuke	before	surprised
what	sought	Mary	scattered
wept	thought	father	together
look	shelf	wished	library
find	proud	nothing	examined
first	kind	instead	enable
class	asleep	garden	reader
school	morning	turned	knowledge

LESSON XXXVI.
More about Little Mary.

1. Mary's father knew nothing about
what she had done. One evening after
this sad experience, her father sat
reading in a room which opened into
the garden.

2. Mary, was no longer able to resist
telling him she was sorry. She came
behind him and gently touched him.
She was waiting to be received as his
favorite girl.

3. Mary told her father, that she had decided not to offend him by being idle, and loving only sweetmeats and play-things. She amused him by giving an account of all the things she had read about, and which she was delighted to find were all true. He told her many other stories of the same kind, with which she was greatly pleased.

4. From that time forth, little Mary was not only the favorite, but the companion of her father. They walked together, and she passed all the time of her holidays in the most pleasant way possible, learning something from everything she saw, and every day becoming wiser and better.

5. When a child receives a present of a book from her father or her mother, the least such a child can do, is to read it carefully through, and keep it in very good order.

6. A good and grateful child will not be satisfied with this. A grateful child will try to gain instruction from the book and improve from reading it.

Questions.—1. Did Mary's father know what she had done? 2. What did Mary tell her father? 3. What kind of a girl was Mary, after this? 4. What will a good child do with books?

long	notice	evening	companion
more	child	whatever	together
told	thing	favorite	possibly
things	least	telling	carefully
read	afford	offend	present
true	herself	giving	receives
with	better	pleased	stories

LESSON XXXVII.

About doing Good at Play.

1. Charles was six years old, and Mary was four. They were nearly of the same size, and they played together.

2. They had several brothers and sisters. Some were older than they, and others were younger. Their parents were poor, and worked hard to get them food to eat, and clothes to wear.

3. These children were often told that they must try all the time to do some good. Charles and Mary thought

they were too young to do much good. When they thought so, they did not try; and when people are not trying to do good, they are apt to do evil. So it was with Charles and Mary.

4. We must tell the truth and say that they were sometimes rude and unkind, and grieved their father and mother. When they felt right, they loved to help their mother to take care of little Ellen and Edward. They would also run to their uncle's and grandfather's on errands. They brought wood for the fireplace when their father was busy.

5. When the weather was good, they went to school. They learned a lot. There was not a school near them. They were too small to travel very far in winter.

6. For this reason, Charles and Mary were home quite often. They thought there was nothing to do. Charles and Mary were not pleased when they were told to do something. They seemed to think they could not do any good for themselves or others.

7. It is wrong to think or feel that way. Their father often told them that they could always do good, when they were kind and pleasant. He said they could do good when they were at play. This seemed very strange to Charles and Mary. They loved to play, but they did not see how it could do any good, except to amuse them.

8. Spell these words, and then I will tell you more.

Questions. —1. What is this story about? 2. What were they told they must try to do? 3. What did Charles and Mary think? 4. Are people apt to do things, when they think they are unable to do them? 5. Did Charles and Mary go to school? 6. Do you go to school? 7. Are you always at school on time?

sisters	loved	Mary	themselves
thought	seemed	always	learned
clothes	nothing	often	sometimes
nearly	Edward	people	weather
brothers	Ellen	pleasant	errands

LESSON XXXVIII.

More about doing Good at Play.

1. Charles and Mary often tried to think what was meant by *doing good at play*. One day they heard their father say that a man was very wicked, who tried to vex others, and make them unhappy.

2. "Now," said Charles, "I know how to do some good when we are at play. Father says it is wicked to vex others and make them unhappy. I know it is good to please them, and make them happy."

3. His father was pleased at this, and called him a good boy. He then told Charles and Mary, that if they were kind and friendly when they were playing, they would soon love to work as well as play, to make others happy.

4. After this, when these little children were at play, they were very

kind. They would never do any thing to vex and trouble others. They would not strike the kitten or puppy, nor pull their hair.

5. One day, when they were busy at play, and were very pleasant and kind, Mary saw that every one seemed happy. They did not make much noise, and so their father could sit and write. Their mother sat in the corner, mending their clothes, and was not disturbed.

6. The older children were at school. Little Ellen and Edward were amused at the play, and prattled about the floor very happily. The kitten thought this was good sport, and ran after the rolling playthings. The puppy showed that he was merry, by twirling around to catch his tail.

7. "See," said Mary, "how much good we do at play. We take good care of little brother and sister, and let father and mother work. We are happy, and make every one happy that sees us."

8. When the older children came home from school, Charles and Mary told them about doing good at play. They had a long talk about it, and all agreed that when they loved each other, and were kind, they could do some good even at play.

9. What is more lovely than a group of innocent little children playing together in love and unity! It reminds me of the little Hymn which says, "Let love through all your actions run, and all your words be mild."

10. Little children should not spend too much time in sport. We enjoy seeing them at play and we take still greater pleasure in seeing them engaged in their studies. Here they will learn that which will make them both useful and happy.

Questions.—1. What did Charles and Mary often try to do? 2. What did Charles say he knew? 3. What did his father say to him? 4. What did Mary see one day? 5. Who were amused at the play? 6. What did they all agree to?

meant	trouble	agreed	wicked
please	busy	father	showed
world	older	mending	rolling
good	happy	prattle	amused
mother	others	running	unhappy
twirling	corner	called	disturbed
playing	about	kitten	finally

LESSON XXXIX.

About the Fox.

1. The fox is about two feet long, and one foot high. He is usually of a light red color. His form is much like the common cur dog, but he has a long bushy tail.

2. We all know that the fox is one of the most knowing and cunning of animals. He is an expert at catching chickens and geese, and all kinds of small birds.

3. There was once a young fox in the town of Reading, England. The fox had been placed at a wheel, and taught to turn the spit, at the kitchen fire. After some time he got tired of cooking dinners for other people to eat, and he escaped to his native woods.

4. Here he met the usual fate of foxes. He was chased by the dogs, and, in his flight, ran through the town of Reading, and springing through the door of his old kitchen, he placed himself at the spit, and resumed his old occupation in the very place where he had been formerly brought up. The dogs did not follow him, and thus he saved his life.

Questions.—1. Can you tell me how long the fox is?   2. How high?   3. What animal does he resemble?   4. For what is the fox remarkable?   5. How did this fox show it?

feet	through	England	springing
from	hungry	dinners	formerly
high	about	cooking	resumed
know	placed	follow	knowing
geese	common	tired	cunning
small	chickens	saved	occupation
ought	kitchen	pretty	usually
knows	Reading	animals	

LESSON XL.
Story about the Lion.

1. The lion is from three to four feet high, and from six to nine feet long.

2. The strength of the lion is very great. He can easily break the skull of a horse by a stroke of his paw. A large lion can drag off an ox.

3. The color of the lion is a yellowish red. He roams about in the forests of Africa and Asia, and is a terror to man and beast. The lion can be tamed, if taken young, and will even show marks of kindness to its keeper. A lion can be very dangerous.

4. In a menagerie at Brussels, there was a cell where a large lion, called Danco, used to be kept. The cell happened to be in need of repair, and the keeper, whose name was William, desired a carpenter to come and mend it. The carpenter came, but he was so afraid of the lion, that he would not go near the cell alone.

5. William entered the cell, and led the lion to the upper part of it, while the other part was being repaired. He played with the animal for some time, but, at last, being tired, both he and the lion fell asleep. The carpenter went on with his work, and when he had finished it, he called out for William to come and see it.

6. He called again and again, but no William answered. The poor carpenter began to be frightened that the lion had made his dinner on the keeper, or else crushed him with his great paws. He crept around to the upper part of the cell, and there, looking through the railing, he saw the lion and William,

sleeping side by side. They were as content as two brothers.

7. He was so astonished, that he uttered a loud cry. The lion, awakened by the noise, started up, and stared at the carpenter with an eye of fury, and then, placing his paw on the breast of his keeper, as if to say, "touch him, if you dare," the heroic beast lay down to sleep again. The carpenter was dreadfully alarmed, and not knowing how he could rouse William, he ran out and told what he had seen.

8. Some people came, and opening the door of the cell, tried to awaken the keeper. He rubbed his eyes, quietly looked around, and expressed himself very well satisfied with his nap. He took the lion's paw, shook it kindly and then left the cell uninjured.

9. The lion sometimes lives to a great age. One by the name of Pompey, died at London in the year 1760 at the age of seventy years.

10. The lion roams about in the forests of Asia and Africa. He utters

a roar which seems like thunder. He stays in places where other animals come for food and drink. When one of them is near enough, he springs upon it with a furious bound.

———————————————

Questions.—1. What is this story about? 2. What feats of strength can the lion perform? 3. What is the color of the lion? 4. Where is the lion found? 5. What is a menagerie? 6. What can you tell me about the lion called Danco? 7. What trait of character did the lion show in this? 8. What trait did the man show? 9. Does any thing useful follow from endangering ourselves in such a way?

stroke	strength	uttered	frightened
break	William	carpenter	character
young	kindness	yellowish	contentedly
railing	Brussels	alarmed	astonished
Danco	Africa	opening	uninjured
lion	brothers	expressed	menagerie
started	sleeping	keeper	

LESSON XLI.
The Boy and Bear.

1. Some time ago, as a boy was going through the woods, he saw a wild and ravenous bear.

2. The boy sprang to the nearest tree, and began to climb with the bear climbing after him.

3. The poor boy made good use of his feet, and soon dashed his enemy to the ground.

4. The bear returned and was again knocked down, carrying with him one of the boy's boots.

5. The bear went up the third time, but with more caution. The young man hoping to escape, climbed up the tree about fifty feet, and as the bear came near, he tried to shake him loose.

6. It was in vain. His boot was held by the paws of the angry animal, which had lost its hold upon the tree, and hung suspended by the poor boy's leg.

7. The boy's strength became exhausted. He let go his hold on the tree, and down they went, boy and bear together, making a tremendous crash among the branches, till they reached the ground.

8. Our hero struck at the bear as he fell eight or ten feet. The frightened boy

and bear sat eyeing each other for some time.

9. The bear was the most severely bruised and was showing no signs of fight. The young man got up and ran away, leaving his boots and hat behind him.

10. His friend with the shaggy coat made no efforts to catch him. The bear cast an ugly look, accompanied by a growl and a shake of the head.

Questions.—1. What is this story about?   2. What did the boy do to get away from the bear?   3. Did the bear follow him?   4. What did the bear get hold of?   5. How do bears usually attack persons?   6. Do you think this boy would have escaped if he had been very much frightened?   7. When we are in danger should we not aim to suppress our fears, so that we do not lose command of our powers?

bear	most	bounded	suspended
time	growl	eyeing	exhausted
since	powers	other	tremendous
sprang	command	merely	becoming
boots	reached	knocked	ravenous
ground	bruised	climbed	infuriated
made	shaggy	carrying	accompanied
down	branches	severely	returned

LESSON XLII.
Pleasing Stories.

1. My little readers have all heard about ghosts, but I suppose they never saw one. A ghost is an imaginary being that some foolish people suppose to walk about at night. Now I need not tell you that there are no such things as ghosts, and nobody need ever expect to see one.

2. People may meet with things they do not exactly understand, and at night, amid the darkness, or by the wavering light of the moon, they may fancy they see strange things. I will tell you one or two stories which will show you how people may be deceived in this way.

3. A boy went out to the barn one night to find the horses. He entered at the great door, and as he was going across the floor, something soft and white seemed to meet him. It drew back, and came toward him again. He was alarmed, and ran toward the door. He looked again and saw the white object moving to and fro.

4. He fancied this to be a ghost, and thought it waved up and down, and seemed to threaten him. He ran to the house in great fear. He told his father that there was a ghost in the barn, that it waved to and fro, that it was white, and was as tall as a giant. It seemed to him to have horns as long as a man's arm!

5. The father got a club, his son Ben got the pitchfork, John took the hoe, Eben the rake, and the mother at the head of this force, with broom in hand, marched out to the barn. They opened the great door, and put in a light. Cautiously they looked around. There, hanging over the floor was a white object, but not a ghost. It was only a white pillow, suspended by a rope. This was used as a swing.

6. Some of the children had been swinging there, and had left the pillow in the swing. The boy who went to find the horses ran against the pillow, and it swung back and forth. He saw it move; he was frightened, and he thought it a ghost as big as a giant!

7. I will tell you another story. A man was going along one dark night. Presently he saw something white before him. He paused. The white object moved along. He pursued it a little. It fled from him, and seemed to stretch out its broad white arms in a threatening manner.

8. The man turned back in fear, and related the story to his friends. There was a man among them who had sense enough not to believe in ghosts. He offered to go to see whether the thing was a real ghost or not. He went with the other man. Pretty soon they came to the spot.

9. There was the white object, sure enough. It moved. They followed. It spread its white arms as before. They followed still faster, and in a moment one of the men caught it. Now what do you think this was? It was only a lame goose!

10. Now let my little readers, if any person ever pretends to have seen a ghost, tell him the story of the pillow and the lame goose.

Questions.—1. What is this story about? 2. What is a ghost? 3. Are there any ghosts now? 4. What mention is made of one in the Bible? 5. What did the man get frightened at? 6. What did the boy get frightened at? 7. How did they make themselves appear by their hasty fear?

heard	threaten	pillow	suspended
ghost	person	against	cautiously
swing	horses	pretends	disbelieved
things	going	moment	understand
marched	moved	turned	threatening
looked	faster	pursued	wavering
seemed	manner	followed	

LESSON XLIII.
The Little Letter Writer.

1. Emily, here is a letter for you. It is from your little cousin John. Hurry, and I will read it to you. How clever it is for cousin John to be able to write a letter! You would like to write a letter, would you not?

2. But you know you cannot write; you have not learned to write yet. I hope you will hurry and learn to read, and then papa will teach you to write.

You want to know when papa will begin to teach you, but that will depend upon yourself.

3. If you take pains, and learn to read all the lessons in this book without stopping to spell a single word, then papa will begin to teach you to write. I shall be very glad when you are able to write a letter to your cousin John in return for this, but we must read it.

4. "Cousin Emily—I am going to tell you about a cat and some rabbits that I have. They all play together in the yard, and sometimes the cat tries to teach the rabbits to catch mice. They will eat together from the same dish.

5. One day they had some beef and bread, and cabbage, set before them on the same plate. The cat agreed that the rabbits might have the cabbage, and Puss took the beef herself. When the cat was eating some bread, the rabbits bit at the other end.

6. Puss did not like that, so she hit the rabbits with her paw. After that, they were very good friends again, and ate it all up. I cannot tell you anything

more about them now, for my hand is tired from writing. I wish you would come here and I will let you see them— This letter is from your cousin, JOHN."

7. Now is not this a very pretty letter, Emily? Should you not like to see Puss and the rabbits playing and eating together?—Yes, I am sure you would. Well, be a good girl, and I will take you someday to see your cousin John and his cat and rabbits.

Questions.—1. What is this story about? 2. Who wrote the letter? 3. To whom did he write? 4. What advantages are there in knowing how to write? 5. Can you write? 6. Would you like to grow up without being able to write?

John	begin	bread	depend
know	agreed	good	clever
your	return	Puss	herself
friends	pretty	learned	together
cousin	about	better	stopping
rabbits	should	eating	lessons
writing	might	cabbage	sometimes

LESSON XLIV.

How the World was made.

1. When we look on the pleasant earth, we see the green grass and the beautiful flowers. We look around us and see the tall trees and the lofty hills. Between them rolls the bright river, and down their sides flow the clear streams.

2. If we raise our eyes when the sky is clear, we look through the light thin air away to where the bright sun is placed, that shines down upon our world to give it light and to make it pleasant.

3. These things were not always so. Six thousand years ago there was no pleasant earth, and then the bright sun was not made. The Great God lived then, and there never was a time when He did not live.

4. When the time came that the Creator was pleased to make this world, He made it all out of nothing. When our world was first created, it had nothing beautiful upon it. It was

all dark and empty. When God wanted light, He said, "Let there be light, and there was light." God made the air that spreads all around our earth. He made the grass to grow, the lovely flowers, the useful herbs, and all the trees that bear the delicious fruit.

5. After all these things were made, the earth was silent as the grave. There were no cattle to eat the grass, or birds, or the smallest insect to fly through the air. When the fourth day came, He made the glorious sun to shine by day, and the moon and stars to give light by night. When the fourth day ended, the sun set upon a silent world. When the fair moon arose and the stars shone in the sky, there was not a man living on all the earth to behold them.

6. The next day came, and the waters brought forth fish, the birds flew through the soft air, and sang among the trees. On the sixth day, God created the beasts of the field. Last of all, He made man in His own image, and breathed into him the breath of life, and man became a living soul.

Questions.—1.What do we see as we look around us?   2. Were these always so? 3. How long is it since the earth was made? 4. By whom was the earth made?   5. What was made on the fourth day?   6. What on the fifth?   7. What on the sixth?   8. What was last made?   9. What is the nobler part of creation?   10. Why is man more noble than the animals and birds?   11. For what should man use these powers?

earth	light	pleased	smallest
look	make	empty	glorious
green	world	breath	behold
tall	around	thousand	waters
trees	empty	created	living
hills	wanted	flowers	breathed

LESSON XLV.
The Bear in a Stage Coach.

1. Two travelers set out from their inn in London, early on a December morning. It was dark as pitch; and one of the travelers not feeling very sleepy, and wishing to talk a little, endeavored to enter into conversation with his neighbor.

2. He accordingly began: "A very dark morning, sir." "Shocking cold weather for travel." "Slow going in these heavy roads, sir."

3. None of these remarks producing a word of answer, the sociable man made one more effort. He stretched out his hands, and feeling of the other's great coat, said—"What a very comfortable coat, sir, you have to travel in!"

4. No answer was made, and the gentleman weary and disgusted with his silent companion, fell into a sound nap, and did not awake until the bright rays of a winter's sun roused him from his slumber.

5. What do you suppose he then saw? It was no more than a great bear, sitting by his side! The creature had a chain over his mouth, so that he could not have talked, even if he had wished to. He was probably a tame bear, and was put into the coach by his owner, who, by some mistake, had remained behind.

6. The traveler readily pardoned his silent companion for not having opened his mouth, and left him without expressing any further astonishment at "the very comfortable coat," which he had on.

Questions.—1. What is this story about? 2. Where did they start from? 3. Where is London?   4. How did the traveler address his companion?   5. Why did he not reply? 6. What is an inn?

mouth	feeling	probably	pardoned
which	suppose	disgusted	readily
sound	creature	December	companion
bright	sitting	travelers	comfortable
owner	further	weather	endeavored
behind	mistake	opened	gentleman
remarks	talked	producing	astonishment

LESSON XLVI.
The Moody Boy.

1. I once knew a little boy who was very naughty, and used to get into a violent mood, and would strike and throw things at his brothers and sister, if they offended him.

2. One day he was playing with his little sister, who did something that did not please him. He ran to the table to break his sister's doll.

3. As he violently caught the doll, he also took up a piece of iron to throw at his sister. Now, it so happened that his mother had just been using the iron, and it was very hot.

4. When the boy caught hold of it, it burned his hand so much that all the skin came off his fingers, and he suffered so much pain that he did not know what to do with himself.

5. Now this little boy did not like to feel pain himself, and yet he was just going to inflict pain upon his sister, by throwing the iron at her.

6. It generally happens when people get into a violent mood, they either do something, or say something, for which they are very sorry afterwards. Besides, violent anger is wicked, and makes a person appear very ferocious.

7. When you are at play, therefore, with your little companions, you should be very careful, and not get angry with them. If you get angry, you cannot enjoy the play any more, and there is great danger that you will hurt some one, for which you will be very sorry.

Questions.—1. What would this little boy sometimes do? 2. Who did something that did not please him? 3. What did he do? 4. What do people do when they get angry?

5. Is it wicked to get angry? 6. What should we do to avoid getting angry?

knew	they	himself	brothers
things	why	almost	sisters
day	ought	little	fingers
please	would	pieces	throwing
once	him	going	mood
throw	doll	always	companion
with	took	mother	offended
break	mighty	inflict	something
and	playing	happens	happened

LESSON XLVII.

The Lost Child and the Gypsies.

1. Gypsies are a class of people who have no settled place to live. They wander about from spot to spot, and sleep at night in tents or in barns. We have no Gypsies in our country, for here every person can find employment of some kind. There is no excuse for idlers and vagrants.

2. In many parts of Europe, the Gypsies are very numerous, and they are often wicked and troublesome. It is said that they are descendants of the Egyptians, and have lived a wandering life ever since the year 1517. At that

time they refused to submit to the Turks, who were the conquerors of Egypt.

3. I have a short story to tell you about these Gypsies. Many years ago, as a boat was putting off, a boy ran along the side of the canal, and wanted a ride. The master of the boat, however, refused to take him, because he had not money enough to pay the usual fare.

4. A rich merchant being pleased with the looks of the boy, whom I shall call Albert, and being touched with compassion towards him, paid the money for him, and ordered him to be taken on board. The little fellow thanked the merchant for his kindness, and jumped into the boat.

5. Upon talking with him afterwards, the merchant found that Albert could readily speak three or four different languages. He also learned that the boy had been stolen away when a child, by a Gypsy, and had rambled ever since, with a gang of these strollers, up and down several parts of Europe.

6. It happened that the merchant, whose heart seems to have inclined towards the boy by a secret kind of instinct, had himself lost a child some years before. The parents, after a long search for him, had concluded that he had been drowned in one of the canals. The mother was so afflicted at the loss of her son, that she died for grief of him.

7. Upon comparing all details, and examining the marks by which the child was described when he was first missing, Albert proved to be the long lost son of the merchant. The lad was well pleased to find a father who was so kind and generous. The father was delighted to see a son return to him whom he had given up for lost.

8. Albert possessed a quick understanding, and in time he rose to eminence, and was much respected for his talents and knowledge. He is said to have visited, as a public minister, several countries in which he formerly wandered as a Gypsy.

Questions.—1. What is this lesson about?   2. What are the Gypsies?   3. Have we any Gypsies in our country?   4. Are there any people in our country who resemble them?   5. Who are they?   6. What feelings did the merchant have towards little Albert?   7. Was it not remarkable that they should have met that way?   8. To whom should they have been grateful for being brought together?   9. Are we apt to forget God's goodness?

grief	lived	concluded	possessed
could	Gypsies	generous	comparing
whom	pleased	inclined	Egyptians
quick	mother	different	understanding
canal	missing	delighted	languages
person	Europe	numerous	compassion
submit	Egypt	afflicted	details

LESSON XLVIII.

Stories about the Monkey.

1. The monkey is a very cunning little animal, and is found in Africa.

2. A lady once had a monkey which had been brought to her from South America, as a present. This monkey,

like all others, was very mischievous, and fond of imitating whatever he saw.

3. His mistress found him one day sitting on her table, holding in one hand a little china mug with water in it, and in the other her toothbrush, with which he was cleaning his teeth, looking all the time in the glass.

4. Her little daughter, Maria, had a large doll, with a very handsome head and face. She one day left this doll in the cradle, and went out of the room. The monkey came in, took the doll in his arms, and jumping upon the washing stand, proceeded to wash its face.

5. He first rubbed it all over with a great quantity of soap; then seizing the towel, he dipped it in the wash bowl, and rubbed it so hard that the doll's face was entirely spoiled because the paint was all washed off.

6. The monkey would sometimes take a fan and fan himself. Once he was found walking up and down the garden, carrying over his head a little parasol, belonging to one of the children.

7. The lady, going one day into her room, saw her new Leghorn Hat walking about the floor. She was at first much surprised, but in a moment she discovered that the monkey was under it. He had taken it out of the bandbox, and when he put it on his head, it of course fell all over him.

8. He was very much frightened when he heard his mistress coming into the room. In trying to get the hat off, he tumbled over it and rolled on the floor, entangled in the ribbons, which were quite spoiled. The hat also was very much broken and damaged.

9. Afraid of being punished, as soon as he got out of the hat, he jumped into the bandbox to hide himself. He sat there trembling, until the lady, who could not help laughing coaxed him to come out, and made him understand that she would not punish him.

10. A large number of monkeys will sometimes assemble in the morning in the woods. One of them will seat himself and begin an oration, while the rest will keep profoundly silent.

11. When he has done they all set up a shout as if for applause, and then the whole assembly breaks up and the monkeys disperse.

Questions.—1. What kind of an animal is a monkey? 2. Who had a monkey that came from South America? 3. Where did she find the monkey one day? 4. What was he doing? 5. What did he do with Maria's doll?

bought	monkey	handsome	frightened
head	mistress	surprised	understand
glass	Leghorn	trembling	discovered
would	laughing	parasol	imitating
putting	jumped	entangled	mischievous
ribbons	walking	proceeded	belonging
fearful	seizing	punished	

LESSON XLIX.
A Pleasing Dialogue.

1. *Samuel.* Now don't, Robert! Do turn him over!

2. *Robert.* For what? It doesn't hurt him to lie so.

3. *Samuel.* Doesn't it hurt him, Robert?

4. *Robert.* No, it doesn't: how can it?

5. *Samuel.* Why, if it did not hurt him, should he stretch his long neck, put out his legs, and make such a scrambling?

6. *Robert.* Oh, I suppose he doesn't like very well to lie on his back, but then it can't hurt him.

7. *Samuel.* But you don't mean to leave him so?

8. *Robert.* Yes, I do.

9. *Samuel.* Oh, Robert! Now you know that would not be right.

10. *Robert.* What do you think I care about a turtle? Come, come, you little boys are always afraid of hurting something or somebody. You must get over these squeamish notions.

11. *Samuel.* Think, Robert. What if you were a turtle, and somebody should put you on your back, so that you could not turn over, and then go off and leave you?

12. *Robert.* Why, I am not a turtle, that is the difference.

13. *Samuel.* But suppose you were. Now tell me, would you like to be treated so?

14. *Robert.* If I were a turtle, I suppose I would not like that.

15. *Samuel.* A turtle can feel. Besides you say yourself that you suppose he doesn't like to lie so. Now tell me, would you like to be treated that way?

16. *Robert.* I suppose I would not. You may go and turn him right side up again, if you choose; I won't.

17. *Samuel.* But I am afraid to touch him!

18. *Robert.* Afraid to touch him! Why he can't hurt you. What are you afraid of? Besides you can take a stick. You need not touch him with you hand.

19. *Samuel.* I would rather you do it.

20. *Robert.* Well, I'll do it, just to please you. You are always so tender of everything, that there's no getting along with you.

21. *Samuel.* You know, Robert, that our parents and our teacher have always told us to treat others as we would wish to be treated, if we were in their place. I am sure if I were a turtle, I should not feel very comfortable, if

some ugly boy should put me on my back, in such a way that I could not turn over again, and then go off and leave me in that position. Nor do I think you would.

Questions.—1. What is this dialogue about? 2. What is a dialogue? 3. What kind of an animal is a turtle? 4. How did Samuel say his parents had told him to treat animals?

mean	neck	teacher	something
thing	always	getting	Samuel
would	again	parents	squeamish
think	besides	Robert	somebody
should	upwards	turtle	yourself
leave	neither	treated	comfortable

LESSON L.

The Quarrelsome Roosters.

1. Here is a story about two foolish roosters that were always quarreling, which is very naughty. You do not quarrel? No, I am glad of it, but if you see any little boys that quarrel, you may tell them the story of the roosters. This is it:

2. There was once a hen who lived in a farmyard, and she had a large brood of chickens. She took very good care of them. She gathered them under her

wings every night, and fed them and nursed them very well.

3. The chickens were all very good, except two roosters that were always quarreling with one another. They were hardly out of the shell before they began to peck at each other; and when they grew larger they fought till they were all bloody.

4. If one picked up a grain of corn, the other always wanted to have it. They never looked pretty because their feathers were pulled off in fighting, until they were quite bare. They pecked at one another's eyes till they were both almost blind.

5. The old hen very often told them how naughty it was to quarrel, but they did not mind her.

6. One day these two roosters had been fighting as they always did. The largest rooster, whose name was Chanticleer, beat the other, and crowed over him, and drove him quite out of the yard.

7. The rooster that had been beaten, slunk away and hid himself, for he was

vexed that he had been conquered. He wanted sadly to be revenged, but he did not know how to manage it, for he was not strong enough himself.

8. After thinking a great deal, he went to an old sly fox that lived near, and said to him, "Fox, if you will come with me, I will show you where there is a large fat rooster in a farmyard, and you may eat him up if you will."

9. The fox was very glad, for he was hungry. He said, "Yes, I will come, with all my heart, and I will not leave a feather of him. Come now, and show me where he may be found."

10. So they went together, and the rooster showed Renard the way into the farmyard. There was poor Chanticleer asleep upon the perch. The fox seized him by the neck, and ate him up, and the other rooster stood by and crowed for joy.

11. When the fox had done, he said, "Chanticleer was very good, but I have not had enough yet;" and so he flew upon the other rooster, and in a moment ate him up too.

Questions.—1. What is this story about? 2. What was the disposition of two of the chickens? 3. Did they foster this quarrelsome disposition? 4. What did it lead them to do? 5. What became of them both? 6. Do people sometimes fall prey to their own craftiness?

how	great	fighting	foolish
slunk	drove	naughty	quarreling
know	yard	thinking	another
there	these	together	bigger
strong	because	perched	always
went	crowed	chickens	feathers
farm	seized	began	himself
heart	showed	looked	Chanticleer

LESSON LI.
Things to be Learned.

1. A bell gives a brisk sound when we strike it with a key, or with a stone, or with a large nail. If we strike a board or the table with a key, it will not give such a sound. A wine glass will also

produce a pretty brisk sound, but if we strike it hard with a nail or a stone, it will break.

2. We hear every sound by means of our ears, which God has formed and placed on each side of our heads, that we might listen to our teachers and be able to talk with one another.

3. The light which flows from the sun consists of seven colors: red, orange, yellow, green, blue, indigo, and violet. The earth is spread over with most of these colors. The fields appear spread over with green, some parts with a light green, and some parts with a dark green color.

4. Fir trees and some poplar trees are dark green. Some roses are red, and some roses are white. The bluebottle flower and some hyacinths, are a blue color.

5. Some daisies are red, some are white, and some have two or three colors. The corn in the fields, the grass in the meadows, and the leaves of trees are green.

6. Iron is heavy, copper is heavier, lead is heaviest. Lead will sink if you throw it into water, but a cork will float on the top of the water. A stone will sink, but wood will float. If you push the wood down with your hand to the bottom of the basin, it will quickly rise again to the top.

7. The sun shines from the heavens and gives us light all the day. It is so bright that we can scarcely look up to it. If we were to look straight towards the sun, it would dazzle our eyes. But if we take a piece of glass that is red or dark green, or a glass that is covered all over with the smoke of a candle, we may look through this glass to the sun without dazzling our eyes.

8. The sun sometimes shines very brightly, and sometimes it is covered with clouds. The sun is giving us light at this moment, but we cannot see it. Can any of you tell the reason why the sun is not seen just now, although it is giving us light? What hides it from our sight?

9. The sky sometimes appears clear, like a large blue dome, or half globe, and sometimes it is covered over with dark clouds. When the sun rises in the east, that part of the sky is often covered with bright red and yellow clouds. When it sets in the evening in the west, the same kind of clouds are sometimes seen.

10. God made the sun, the moon, and the stars. He also made the fields, the trees, and the corn. He formed our bodies and our souls. He gave us eyes to see with, ears that we may hear, hands to handle with, feet to walk with, and He preserves us every moment.

11. He is present with us in this place, and sees all that we do, though we cannot see Him. Let us give thanks to God, for He is good. Let us do what He commands.

Questions.—1. What gives a brisk sound? 2. Of how many colors does light consist? 3. What are those colors? 4. How may we look at the sun without pain? 5. Who made the sun, the moon, and the stars?   6. What should we do to show that we are thankful for His goodness?

straight	reduce	forwards	scarcely
shines	teachers	evening	dazzling
clouds	colors	cannot	sometimes
white	bottom	moment	giving
break	candle	basin	comfort
might	present	towards	flowers
throw	handle	quickly	poplar
wood	produce	reason	meadows

LESSON LII.
About Oranges.

1. The orange is a round yellow friut, of delicious flavor, and is about as large as a large apple.

2. Oranges grow in great quantities in the southern part of the United States. This fruit is also raised perfectly in the West Indies.

3. Great quantities are also brought from Seville, in Spain, and from the Island of Malta, in the Mediterranean.

4. Most of the oranges intended to be sent away are gathered while they are still green. They are then carefully wrapped with brown paper, and put into boxes.

5. The orange tree has an upright smooth trunk, and smooth shining leaves. An oil is obtained from the flowers of the tree, and forms a perfume which is very agreeable.

6. The shaddock (large grapefruit) is a species of the orange, but much larger. It is a native of China, where the name "sweet ball" is given it.

7. There are many varieties of this fruit. Some have a white pulp, others have red. Some are sweet, and some are sour.

———————

Questions.—1. Where do oranges grow? 2. How are they packed for exportation? 3. What is obtained from the flowers of the orange tree? 4. What is the usual size of an orange?

round	green	quantities	gathered
great	oranges	delicious	perfection
fruit	carefully	agreeable	
Mediterranean			

LESSON LIII.

Stories about Birds.

1. It is known by almost all children who have ever seen a parrot, that birds of that species may be taught to speak many words, almost as distinctly as a child.

2. Parrots are sometimes hung up in a cage by the door of a shop where goods are sold. They are taught to speak to persons passing along the

street, to ask them to walk in. In some instances, where candy and sugar-plums are kept for sale they are taught to tell little boys and girls how many plums they may have for a cent.

3. I was once walking along in one of the streets of the city when my attention was drawn towards a voice that I heard, not far behind me. It was singing out very loudly and quite distinctly, the first line of the little Scotch song,

"Oh, dear! what can the matter be?"

4. I looked in the direction of the voice and saw that it came from an old parrot, hanging in his cage, at the door of a French woman who sold apples, and raisins, and oranges.

5. But there are other sorts of birds, much prettier than parrots, quite as docile, and much more interesting. I mean those beautiful little singing birds, such as linnets and canary birds, which are kept in cages in parlors on account of their cheerfulness and the sweetness of their song.

6. These little birds are sometimes carried around for exhibition, after they have been taught to perform a great many of their amusing and very astonishing feats.

7. In these exhibitions, I have seen linnets pretend to be dead, and remain perfectly tranquil, and unmoved, when small cannons were fired, within an inch of their bodies, from a little wooden fort.

———————

Questions.—1. What is this story about? 2. What can parrots do? 3. What have they been known to say? 4. Do parrots understand what they say? 5. Why are they not able to understand, if they can talk? 6. Who are sometimes like parrots?

known	raising	pretend	themselves
street	after	cannons	exhibition
child	about	singing	cheerfulness
first	perform	woman	interesting
almost	persons	creatures	proceeded
walking	linnets	wooden	astonishing
immoral	distinctly		

LESSON LIV.

More Stories about Little Birds.

1. The canary bird is so named because it was first brought from the Canary Islands. It is a very beautiful little bird, and will often become very much attached to the person to whom it belongs.

2. The canary bird may be taught to perch upon your shoulder, and feed from your hand. It is wonderful how many things it may be taught to do.

3. A Frenchman, not many years ago, exhibited some canary birds in London, which performed several very amusing tricks, which one would hardly believe if he had not seen them.

4. One of them would take a slender stick in its claws, pass its head between its legs, and allow itself to be turned round, as a bird is when the cook is roasting it.

5. Another balanced itself, and was swung backwards and forwards on a kind of slack rope. A third allowed itself to be shot at, and falling down as if dead, was put into a little wheelbarrow, and wheeled away by one of his comrades.

6. Partridges have also been taught to play the part of artillerymen. At the word of command, from their teacher, they would light their matches at a little brass furnace. At the second command they would touch off the cannon at the noise of which they did not seem in the least frightened.

7. At another signal, some of the little warriors fell on their sides and

pretended to be dead; some limped away as if they were lame; and others cried out as if they had been wounded. At the slightest roll of the drum, the dead partridges jumped up, and cripples recovered the use of their limbs, and all were as lively and happy as ever.

Questions.—1. Where are canary birds brought from? 2. Where are the Canary Islands? 3. What did the Frenchman teach his canary birds? 4. Who are Frenchmen? 5. What have partridges been taught to do? 6. Do you think it right to catch little birds and keep them shut up in a cage? 7. How would you like to be confined in a little golden prison?

taught	down	between	artillery
swing	jumped	command	recovered
much	French	wounded	exhibited
whom	matches	balanced	pretended
which	signal	suffered	wonderful
round	cripples	attached	partridges
stack	lively	London	performed

LESSON LV.

Spring, Summer, Autumn and Winter.

1. How mild and fine is spring! The rose puts forth its leaves. The fruit-trees are in full bloom. The snowdrop grows up at our feet. Sweet scents float on the soft breeze.

2. Come, Charles and Ann, and let us walk upon the green grass. Listen! What hum do we hear? It is a hive of bees; how busy they are! The bees sip their sweets from the flowers, they form small cells with wax. They toil all the days that are fair, but when it is cold, they keep close to their hives.

3. The vine climbs up the high wall; the hop clings around the tall poles. The rose, though so sweet, has a thorn. The bee with its sweets has a sting.

4. Summer has now come, and the cold dews have left the earth. Now the high sun darts his beams. The flocks and herds seek the cool shade. The fruits are now red on the trees. The meadows are thick with high grass.

5. The sweet hay scents the vale. The men and boys spread the hay. Let us help to toss the new mown grass. Let us sit down on the new made hay.

6. The cool stream winds through the vale, and the beautiful barge skims down the stream. Soft sounds float on the still air. Let us sit down in the cool shade. Then we will go home through the grove.

7. See, the trees bend with the ripe fruit of autumn. The wheat looks bright like gold. The ears are now ripe on the stem; they bend down the stalk. The ears are full of ripe wheat.

8. The men now reap the high grain; then they tie it up in large heaps. See how thick the sheaves stand. The team goes home with the load.

9. See the stacks in the farmyard. The large barns are full of grain. Let us sit down near the stacks. The woods ring with the voice of joy. The glad farmer, nearby, views his spacious barns filled with various grain.

10. Stern winter has now come, and the frost is hard on the ground.

"Charles, call James and Ann to me. Where are your hats and coats? Let us walk around the fields."

11. The trees are now stripped of their leaves. The birds sit still on the boughs. The ice hangs from the high roof; the snow and ice shine in the sun. See, the boys and men slide and skate on the ice which covers the pond.

12. Listen! Do you hear the sound of the horn, the yelping of the hounds, and the gun? Now I feel for the poor birds, the squirrels and the rabbits.

Questions.—1. What is this lesson about? 2. What is said of spring? 3. When does spring begin? 4. When does it end? 5. When does summer begin? 6. When does it end? 7. When does autumn begin? 8. When does it end? 9. When does winter begin? 10. When does it end? 11. How are the different seasons occasioned? 12. By what are the seasons distinguished from each other?

sheaves	Charles	hounds	stripped
there	James	where	spacious
comes	stream	wheat	yelping
steam	floats	nearer	summer
shines	grove	prospect	autumn
spices	grain	squirrels	winter

LESSON LVI.

The Honest Boy and the Thief.

1. Charles was an honest boy, but his neighbor, Jack Pilfer, was a thief. Charles would never take anything for his own which did not belong to him; but Jack would take whatever he could get. When he found anything that was lost, he would never restore it to the owner.

2. Early one summer's morning, as Charles was going to school, he met a man opposite the public house who had oranges to sell. The man wished to stop and get his breakfast, and asked Charles if he would hold his horse while he went into the house.

3. He first asked the landlord if he knew Charles to be an honest boy, as he would not like to trust his oranges with him, if he were not.

4. "Yes," said the landlord, "I have known Charles all his life, and have never known him to lie or steal. All the neighbors know him to be an honest boy, and I believe your oranges will be

as safe with him as with yourself."

5. The orange man then put the bridle into Charles' hand, and went into the house to eat his breakfast.

6. Very soon Jack Pilfer came along the road. Seeing Charles holding the horse, he asked him whose horse he had there, and what was in the baskets on the horse. Charles told him that the owner of the horse was in the house, and that there were oranges in the baskets.

7. As soon as Jack found there were oranges in the baskets, he was determined to have one. Going up to the basket, he slipped in his hand and took out one of the largest and was making off with it.

8. But Charles said, "Jack, you shall not steal these oranges while I have the care of them, and so you may just put that one back into the basket."

9. "Not I," said Jack, "as I am the largest, I shall do as I please." Charles was not afraid of him. Taking the orange out of Jack's hand, he threw it back into the basket.

10. Jack then attempted to go around to the other side and take one from the other basket; but as he stepped too near the horse's heels, he received a violent kick which sent him sprawling to the ground.

11. His cries soon brought the people out of the house. When they learned what had happened, they said that Jack got what he deserved. The orange man, taking Charles' hat, filled it with oranges. He said Charles had been so faithful in guarding them, he should have all these for his honesty.

Questions.—1. What is this story about? 2. Which was the honest boy? 3. What kind of a boy was Jack Pilfer? 4. What is a landlord? 5. What kind of a reputation did the landlord give Charles? 6. How can boys secure a good name? 7. What advantage is there in possessing a good reputation?

wrought	should	bridle	summer
found	these	engage	sprawling
whose	round	seeing	landlord
school	honest	neighbor	determined
horse	sewed	largest	happened
hand	owner	guarding	honesty

LESSON LVII.

True Courage.

1. One cold winter's day, three boys were passing by a schoolhouse. The oldest was a mischievous fellow, always in trouble himself, and trying to get others into trouble. The youngest, whose name was George, was a very amiable boy.

2. George wished to do right, but was very much lacking in moral courage. The other boys were named Henry and James. As they were walking along, the following dialogue took place.

3. *Henry.*—What fun it would be to throw a snowball against the school-room door, and make the teacher and students all jump!

4. *James.*—You would jump, if you did that. If the teacher did not catch you and whip you, he would tell your

father, and you would get a whipping then. That would make you jump higher than the students, I think.

5. *Henry.*—Why, we could get so far off, before the teacher could come to the door, that he could not tell who we are. Here is a snowball just as hard as ice, and George had as soon throw it against that door as not.

6. *James.*—Give it to him and see. He would not dare to throw it against the door.

7. *Henry.*—Do you think George is a coward? You don't know him as well as I do. Here, George, take this snowball, and show James that you are not such a coward as he thinks you are.

8. *George.*—I am not afraid to throw it, but I do not want to. I do not see that it will do any good, or that there will be any fun in it.

9. *James.*—There! I told you he would not dare to throw it.

10. *Henry.*—Why, George, are you turning coward? I thought you did not fear anything. We shall have to call you chicken-hearted. Come, save your

reputation and throw it. I know you are not afraid to.

11. *George.*—"Well, I am not afraid to," said George. "Give me the snowball. I would as soon throw it as not."

12. Whack! went the snowball against the door; and the boys took to their heels. Henry was laughing as heartily as he could to think what a fool he had made of George.

13. George afterwards got a whipping for his folly, as he richly deserved. He was such a coward that he was afraid of being called a coward. He did not dare to refuse to do as Henry told him to, because he was afraid that he would be laughed at.

14. If he had been really a brave boy, he would have said, "Henry, do you suppose that I am such a fool as to throw that snowball, just because you want that? You may throw your own snowballs, if you please."

15. Henry would perhaps have tried to laugh at him. He would have called him a coward, hoping in this way to persuade him to obey his wishes.

16. George would have replied, "Do you think that I care for your laughing? I do not think it is right to throw a snowball against the school-room door. I will not do that which I think is wrong, if the whole town joins with you in laughing."

17. This would have been real moral courage. Henry would have seen at once that it would do no good to laugh at a boy who had so bold a heart. You must have this fearlessness of spirit, or you will be continually involved in trouble, and will deserve and receive contempt.

18. There will be occasions when it will require a severe struggle to preserve your integrity. Always remember that if you would do any good in the world, you must possess this moral courage. It is the lack of this that leaves thousands to live in a way which their consciences disapprove, and to die in despair.

19. Without possessing this trait of character, to some considerable degree, no one will ever become a Christian.

You must learn to act for yourself, unintimidated by the censure, and unmoved by the flattery of others.

———————————

Questions.—1. What is this lesson about? 2. Where were the boys going? 3. What did Henry think would be fun? 4. Didn't such a thought show that he was a mischievous boy?   5. What means did they devise to get George to throw it?   6. Don't persons often do wrong rather than be ridiculed?   7. Didn't George show his lack of courage in throwing the ball? 8. What would have been true courage?

against	before	laughing	undecided
afraid	little	talking	independence
always	father	different	happened
courage	moral	instructor	considerable
express	George	flattery	mischievous
perhaps	James	opinion	fearlessness
persons	Henry	induced	unintimidated

LESSON LVIII.
Young Soldiers.

1. Oh, were you never a schoolboy,
   And did you never train,
   And feel that swelling of the heart
   You never can feel again?
   Did you never meet, far down
                         the street,
   With plumes and banners gay,
   While the kettle, for the kettledrum
   Played your march, march away?

2. It seems to me but yesterday,
   Nor scarce so long ago

Since we shouldered our muskets
  To charge the fearful foe.
Our muskets were of cedar wood,
  With ramrod bright and new;
With bayonet forever set,
  And painted barrel, too.

3. We charged upon a flock of geese,
    And put them all to flight,
Except one sturdy gander
    That thought to show us fight;
But, ah, we knew a thing or two;
    Our captain wheeled the van—
We routed him, we scouted him,
    Nor lost a single man.

4. Our captain was as brave a lad
    As ever commission bore;
All brightly shone his new tin
                            sword,
    A paper cap he wore.
He led us up the steep hillside,
    Against the western wind,
While the cockerel plume that
                    decked his head
Streamed bravely out behind.

5. We shouldered arms, we carried
arms,
We charged the bayonet;
And woe unto the mullein stalk
That in our course we met.
At two o'clock the roll we called,
And to the close of day,
With our brave and plumed
captain,
We fought the mimic fray,—
Till the supper bell, from out the
dell,
Bade us march, march away.

———————————— ∙∙ ————————————

Questions.—1. What is this lesson written in—prose or poetry? 2. What is poetry? 3. What is prose? 4. Why do persons write in poetry rather than in prose? 5. What is this story about?

commission	bayonets	decked	plumed
shouldered	scouted	mimic	carried
cockerel	wheeled	captain	charged

LESSON LIX.
The Reindeer and the Rabbit.

MARY.

1. I wish I were a reindeer
   To gallop over the snow;
   Over frosty Lapland drear,
   So merrily I'd go.

ANN.

2. A little rabbit I would be,
   With fur so soft and sleek,
   And timid ears raised prettily,
   And looks so very meek.

MARY.

3. But then perhaps some cruel rat,
   Would find your burrow out;
   Or the furious old grey cat
   Might scratch your peepers out.

ANN.

4. 'Tis true they might, but don't
      you know
   The reindeer's wretched lot?
   His dinner and his bed is snow,
   And supper he has not.

MARY.

5. But then he is so useful, Ann;
   His masters love him so!
   Dear creatures, they do all they
      can,
   And are content with snow.

———————

Questions.—1. What did Mary wish?   2.
What is a reindeer?   3. What was Ann's
wish?   4. What is a rabbit?   5. Why are you
better than a rabbit or reindeer?

know	burrow	reindeer	haughty
scratch	gallop	wretched	Lapland
content	perhaps	furious	clover
dinner	rabbit		

LESSON LX.
About the Globe.

1. You have heard that a long time
ago, Columbus, who lived on the other
side of the world, thought it was round.
When he sailed a great way over the
sea, he found the country that we live
in; and since then, a great many vessels
have been sailed around the world.

2. We know the earth is round because we can see so much farther off when we get on some mountain, or high above the earth. The water, too, is of a round shape. When sailors are at sea and want to look far over the ocean, they climb high up the mast of the ship to see a great distance.

3. If we could fly away off and stand on the moon, we might look at this world, and it would seem just like a large bright moon in the sky. As we looked upon it, and the bright clouds passed by it, it would seem to hang there, or move along, as the moon now appears to us who live on the earth.

4. The moon, and the sun, and the stars look small, because they are far away. The moon is two hundred and forty thousand miles from our world, and the sun is about ninety-five millions of miles. Nearly all the stars are at so very great a distance that nobody can find out how far they are from us.

5. You know that yesterday we sent off a beautiful balloon. When near to

us, it looked as large as a great wagon cover, but as it moved away through the air, it seemed to become smaller and smaller. In a short time, it looked like a little bright speck in the blue sky, and then it was lost in the clouds. The great worlds of light that are seen in the sky only look small, because they are so very far away.

6. We can only see a short distance, and a little of our world at once. We could not see the greater part of it if we were to travel as long as we live. The earth is as round as this ball, and it is almost eight thousand miles through from one side to the other. It is nearly twenty-five thousand miles all around.

7. Nobody has found out what there is several miles in the ground, but we know there are upon the earth hills and mountains, plains and woods, and large rivers, lakes and oceans. There are seven or eight hundred millions of people living on the world, and millions of millions of other creatures living on the earth, and in the air, and in the waters.

8. Some part of the earth is always warm, and has only summer, and some parts are mostly pleasant, and there are four seasons, as we have in our country. The seasons are called spring, summer, autumn, and winter.

9. There are some places toward the north and south poles, where it is always very cold, and where hardly anything grows. There are long nights for nearly half the year, and then a day comes and is just as long.

10. The Lord has been very good to us to place us in a part of the earth where we have such pleasant seasons. The days and nights are just long enough, if we employ our time as we should. If this world were made more delightful to us than it is, and we never had any trouble here, we might wish to live here always.

———————

Questions.—1. Who first came to this country from over the sea?   2. What is the form of the earth?   3. How would our earth appear if seen from the moon?   4. How far is the sun from us?   5. How far is the moon? 6. How many seasons do we have? 7. What are they called? 8. Who is it that has created so many things for our happiness?

round	man	small	sailed
world	been	morn	lived
time	great	most	wagon
heard	since	high	above
away	water	because	farther
mountain	thousand	smaller	people
distance	millions	looked	other
hundred	ninety	greater	river
forty	nearly	almost	seven

LESSON LXI.

The Little Boy and the Hatchet.

1. Never, perhaps, did a parent take more pains than did the father of General Washington to inspire his son George with an early love of Truth. "Truth, George," said he, "is the most lovely quality of youth. I would ride fifty miles, my son, to see the boy whose heart is so honest, and whose lips so pure, that we may depend on every word he says.

2. "How lovely does such a child appear in the eyes of everybody! His

parents dote on him. His relations glory in him. They praise him before their children, and wish them to follow his example. They often invite him to visit them, and when he comes, they receive him with joy, and treat him as one whose visits they enjoy most.

3. "But oh, George, how far from this is the case with the boy who is given to lying! Good people avoid him wherever he goes, and parents dread to see him in company with their children.

4. "Oh, George, my son, rather than see you come to this pass, dear as you are to me, gladly would I assist to nail you up in your little coffin, and follow you to your grave.

5. "Hard, indeed, it would be to me to give up my son, whose feet are always so ready to run about with me, and whose smiling face and sweet prattle make so large a part of my happiness. But still I would give him up, rather than see him a common liar."

6. "Father," said George, with tears in his eyes, "do I ever tell lies?"

7. "No, George: I thank God you do not, my son; and I rejoice in the hope you never will. Whenever by accident you do anything wrong, which must often be the case, as you are but a little boy yet, you must never say what is not true to conceal it, but come bravely up, my son, like a little man, and tell me of it."

8. When George was about six years old, he was made the owner of a little hatchet, with which he was much pleased, and went about chopping everything that came in his way. One day, when in his garden, he unluckily tried the edge of his hatchet on the body of a fine young English cherry tree, which he barked so badly that he destroyed it.

9. The next morning, the old gentleman, finding out what had befallen his favorite tree, came into the house, and angrily asked who had destroyed the tree. Nobody could tell him anything about it. At this moment in came George, with his hatchet.

10. "George," said his father, "do you know who killed that fine cherry tree in the garden?" This was a hard question. George was silent for a moment, and then, looking at his father, his young face bright with conscious love of truth, he bravely cried out, "I can't tell a lie, father. You know, I can't tell a lie. I did cut it with my hatchet."

11. "Come to my arms, my dearest boy!" cried his father, happily; "come to my arms! You killed my cherry tree, George, but you have now paid me for it a thousand fold. Such proof of heroic truth in my son is of more value than a thousand trees, though they were all of the purest gold."

Questions.—1. What is this story about? 2. Who was George Washington? 3. What did Mr. Washington take great pains to do? 4. Did George attempt to conceal what he had done? 5. How did his father feel toward him when he made his confession? 6. When we have done wrong, what are we tempted to do? 7. What may we expect by confessing our faults?

pains	receive	looking	happiness
comes	appear	finding	befallen
youth	owner	favorite	gentleman
dread	author	accident	whenever
coffin	pleased	general	transports
invite	dearest	relations	thousand
lying	question	nobody	Washington

LESSON LXII.
The Lord's Prayer.

1. Our Father in heaven
    We hallow they name!
  May thy kingdom holy
    On earth be the same!
  O, give to us daily
    Our portion of bread,
  It is from thy bounty
    That all must be fed.

2. Forgive our transgressions,
    And teach us to know
  That humble compassion
    That pardons each foe;
  Keep us from temptation,
    From weakness and sin,
  And thine be the glory
    Forever—Amen!

Questions.—1. What is it to hallow the name of the Lord? 2. From whom do we receive our daily bread? 3. If God should neglect to supply us with food, what would become of us? 4. How can we show our gratitude to God for his continued kindness?

thine	forgive	Father	kingdom
bread	pardon	heaven	weakness
teach	daily	humble	compassion
earth	glory	forever	temptations
same	Amen	hallow	transgressions

LESSON LXIII.
Mother, what is Death?

CHILD.

1. "Mother, how still the baby lies!
    I cannot hear his breath;
   I cannot see his laughing eyes,—
    They tell me this is death.

2. "My little work I thought to bring,
    And sat down by his bed,
   And pleasantly I tried to sing,—
    They hushed me—he is dead!

3. "They say that he again will rise,
   More beautiful than now;
That God will bless him in the
                               skies—
   O, mother, tell me how!"

MOTHER.

4. "Daughter, do you remember, dear,
   The cold, dark thing you brought,
And laid upon the casement here,—
   A withered worm, you thought?

5. "I told you, that Almighty power
   Could break that withered shell,
And show you, in a future hour,
   Something would please you well.

6. "Look at that chrysalis my love—
   An empty shell it lies;
Now raise your wondering glance
                               above,
   To where yon insect flies!"

CHILD.

7. "O, yes, mama! how very gay,
   Its wings of starry gold!
And see! it lightly flies away
   Beyond my gentle hold.

8. "O, mother! now I know full well,
    If God that worm can change,
And draw it from this broken cell,
    On golden wings to range—

9. "How beautiful will brother be,
    When God shall give him wings,
Above this dying world to flee,
    And live with heavenly things!"

Question.—1. What is this piece of poetry about?   2. Where did the little girl go and sit?   3. What was she going to do?   4. Will little children be raised from the dead?   5. From what book do we learn this?   6. Where must we all appear after we are raised from the dead?   7. Of what shall we then be judged?

change	starry	lightly	beautiful
worm	gentle	away	wondering
thought	broken	mama	chrysalis
glance	empty	hushed	something
things	insect	withered	casement
world	future	brother	remember
above	power	daughter	heavenly
dying	golden	laughing	pleasantly
going	mother		

LESSON LXIV.
The Disobedient Girl.

1. Two good little girls, named Emily and Frances, lived very near to each other. They were cousins, but they loved each other almost as well as sisters.

2. Both of them loved to do as their parents wished, and they were neat, orderly, and industrious. They also loved their books, and were always on time with good lessons at the Sabbath School, and the weekday school.

3. Their teacher said that Emily and Frances were very obedient, and were very studious. The minister said that they were silent and serious when they were at church.

4. Their good behavior gave great comfort to their parents. Nothing else made Emily and Frances so happy as to see that their parents were satisfied with their conduct. I hope that all the children who read this story will find equal pleasure in making their parents happy.

5. There was another little girl, called Jane, who lived a short distance from Emily and Frances. She was not like them, but was full of sly tricks, and loved mischief, and did not obey her father and mother.

6. Jane was never happy; and, if she saw others happy, she loved to disturb them. Wicked persons are very apt to be envious. They are displeased when they see others enjoy blessings which are given them.

7. One fine afternoon in the summer, when there was no school, the good little girls had permission to take their dolls and some other playthings, and sit under a shady tree, a little way from the house.

8. Their mothers told them to keep still in the shade, because the heat was very great. They were also told not to go farther than the great tree, for there might be a shower; and if they were far from the house, they might get wet, and be sick.

9. Emily and Frances had not been playing very long, when Jane came up

to them, and asked what they were doing. They answered her pleasantly and kindly, but she said, "It is silly to sit under this tree; come with me into the forest, and you will have a good time, picking flowers and berries."

10. They told Jane what their parents had said, and asked her to stay and play with them, but she refused. She said her mother had told her the same thing, but that she knew it never rained when the sun shone so brightly.

11. Frances said that she did not think Jane would speak so, if she remembered the commandment, "Honor thy father and thy mother."

12. Jane said she did not remember it, and did not care for it. "Come," said she, "let's go down to the meadow among the haystacks," and away she ran. Jane soon came to a fence, and in getting over, her frock caught, and she fell head first to the earth.

13 .The girls heard her cries, and came to her aid, but poor Jane would not be comforted. She knew she had done wrong—she had torn her frock,

her face was covered with blood, and now she dreaded to meet her mother, in case she should again be punished for her disobedience. She wanted the girls to leave her and she would go home another way.

Questions.—1. What is this story about?   2. Who were the good girls? 3. What was Jane's character?   4. Where were Emily and Frances playing one afternoon?   5. What did Jane want them to do?   6. What had their parents told them? 7. What did she do?   8. What happened to her?   9. What may children expect who disobey their parents?

disturb	Frances	naughty	behavior
enjoy	Emily	trouble	industrious
about	cousins	minded	afternoon
befall	wished	studious	answered
asked	picking	satisfied	pleasantly
sorry	flowers	serious	remembered
kindly	berries	envious	commandment

LESSON LXV.

More about the Disobedient Girl.

1. Jane had not been gone long, before some black clouds arose in the northwest. They were soon overhead, and the lightning flashed from them, and the thunder was terribly loud.

2. The birds flew about, as though greatly alarmed, and hid under the shed, and in the barns. The cattle ran and bellowed about the fields, as if filled with terror. Birds and animals seem to know when a storm is coming, and what kind of a storm it will be, much better than men.

3. Emily and Frances hurried home, and had just reached their house when the wind blew and whirled furiously, and the rain came down in torrents. Large hailstones also fell, and beat down the grass and grain, and broke the windows which were not covered with blinds.

4. These good little girls were then very glad and thankful that they were

safe at home, but they thought of Jane, and of her poor mother. They told their parents all that Jane said and did, and as soon as anyone could safely go out, a man was sent to tell her father and mother where she was.

5. Her father went into the wood, and looked a long time for Jane. At last he found her with her clothes completely wet, and her head, neck, and arms sadly bruised by the hail. She was sitting under a tree, and was so beaten and frightened, that she did not try to move.

6. When her father took her home, her mother did all that she could to prevent her taking cold; but the naughty girl had been so long wet with the rain, which was made cold by the hail, that she was very chilled. The next day she was quite sick, and the bruises made her very sore and lame.

7. For several weeks it was thought that Jane would never be well again. But at last she grew better, and then she told her kind mother that she would try to be a good child.

8. Jane kept her promise, but it was a long time before she got over her bad habits. When she had learned to fear the Lord, and to honor her father and mother, she was very happy.

9. When I last saw her, she was sitting with Emily and Frances under the same tree where she had treated them so badly. They were now all good friends, and they were telling how happy it made them to keep the FIFTH COMMANDMENT.

Questions.—1. Where did Emily and Frances now hurry to? 2. Why were they glad when they got home? 3. Where did Jane's father go? 4. When Jane was brought home what took place? 5. What causes all this sickness and pain? 6. Did Jane afterwards become a good girl? 7. What did she then remember? 8. What is the Fifth Commandment?

loud	mother	promise	northwest
grass	reached	hastened	completed
grain	whirled	covered	furiously
their	thankful	Frances	naughty
greatly	telling	Emily	frightened
houses	bruised	windows	learned
father	taking	reaching	commandment

LESSON LXVI.

Emulation without Envy.

1. Frank's father was speaking to a friend one day on the subject of competition at school. He said that he was sure that envy is not the necessary result of competition at school.

2. He had been excelled by many, but he could not remember ever having felt envious of his successful rivals. "Nor did my winning many a prize from my friend Birch ever lessen his friendship for me."

3. In support of the truth of what Frank's father had said, a friend, who was present, related an anecdote, which he had observed in a school in his neighborhood.

4. At this school, the sons of several wealthy farmers, and others, who were poorer, received instruction. Frank listened with great attention while the gentleman gave the following account of the two rivals.

5. "It happened that the son of a rich farmer, and of a poor widow, came

in competition for the head of their class. They were so nearly equal, that the teacher could scarcely decide between them. Some days one, and some days the other, gained the head of the class. It was determined by seeing who should be at the head of the class for the greater number of days in the week.

6. "The widow's son, by the last day's trial won, and maintained his place the following week, until the school was dismissed for the vacation or holidays.

7. "When they met again, the widow's son did not appear, and the farmer's son being next in excellence, could now have been at the head of his class. Instead of seizing the vacant place, however, he went to the widow's house to ask why her son was absent.

8. "Poverty was the cause. She found that she was not able, no matter how hard she tried, to continue to pay for his tuition and books, and the poor boy had returned to day labor for her support.

9. "The farmer's son, out of the allowance of pocket money which his father gave him, bought all the necessary books and paid for the tuition of his rival. He also permitted him to be brought back again to the head of his class, where he continued for a long time, at the expense of his generous rival."

10. Frank clapped his hands at hearing this story. Mary came up to ask what pleased him so much, and he repeated it to her with delight. "That farmer's boy," added he, "must have had a strong mind, for my father's friend, who told the anecdote, said that people of strong minds are never envious; that weak minds are the ones filled with envy."

Questions. —1. What is the subject of this lesson? 2. What is emulation? 3. What is envy? 4. Do you think it necessary to be envious in order to emulate? 5. Do you think the farmer's son was motivated by feelings of envy? 6. Shouldn't all children aim to make higher and higher attainments?

Frank	brought	endeavors	consequences
friend	scarcely	happened	competition
could	envious	returned	determined
strong	winning	poverty	maintained
much	speaking	anecdote	considerable
inquire	wealthy	asserted	observation
widow	support	successful	necessary
seeing	continue	recollect	gentleman
farmer	victory	continued	dismissed
pocket	fallen	allowance	instruction
money	ensuing		

LESSON LXVII.

Story about George Washington.

1. George Washington's father one day prepared a bed of earth in the garden near George's favorite walk.

2. In this he wrote, with a small stick, the name of his son, "George Washington," at full length, and filled the letters with cabbage seed.

3. After he had done this, he carefully smoothed over the bed, and waited for the seed to come up.

4. In a few days the plants appeared, and there was to be seen, in living green—in nature's own writing—the name of "George Washington."

5. As George was taking his favorite walk in the garden, either trundling his wagon or riding his prancing horse, his eye caught sight of the wonder.

6. He stopped and gazed—he spelled the name—he hesitated and doubted, and read again. He never saw such a wonder before—he never heard of any such thing—could not believe his eyes; yet it was so.

7. He didn't stay long but bounded away towards the house, and soon stood in the presence of his father.

8. "Father!" exclaimed he.

9. "Well, George, what's the matter?"

10. "Why, father, I've seen such a sight!"

11. "What? Where, my son?" inquired Mr. Washington.

12. "In the garden, sir."

13. "And what have you seen strange in the garden?"

14. "Oh, come and see—come and see, father; something I never heard of before," said George.

15. Mr. Washington went with unusual readiness to the spot, well convinced what the strange sight would prove to be. George led the way by some rods.

16. "Here, father, here it is; did you ever see such a strange sight before?"

17. "What is it you see so strange?" said Mr. Washington, now drawing near, and appearing somewhat surprised.

18. "Why, here, father, don't you see these?" said George, stooping down and passing his little fingers over the letters of his name in the bed.

19. "What? George."

20. "Why, my name, father—here—growing in this bed, so green. How did it happen?"

21. "Is it anything wonderful?" asked Mr. Washington.

22. "Why, father, I never heard of any such thing before, did you?"

23. "Why—George—well"—said Mr. Washington, hesitating at the unexpected question, "it certainly is curious."

24. "But, father, how did it get here?"

25. "May be, by *chance*, George."

26. "No, no, father, it could not have come by chance. I never heard of such a thing."

27. "Well, and why may it not have come by chance?"

28. "I don't know, father, but I don't *believe* it did."

29. "There are many things we don't believe, George, which, nevertheless are true."

30. "Yes, yes, father, but I never *saw* any like it before."

31. "That may be, and yet it may have come by chance."

32. "Well, I never *heard* of any such thing."

33. "True, and yet might it not happen, although *you* never heard of it?"

34. "Ah, but, father, how should little plants grow up just so as to make the letters of *my* name—*all* the letters—all in *exact order*? Why was it not *your name*? Ah, father, why was it anyone's name?"

Questions.—1. What is this story about? 2. What did Mr. Washington plant? 3. How did he plant them? 4. How did George feel when he discovered his name? 5. Was it a very novel sight?

said	earth	exact	wonderful
all	green	father	appearing
such	name	fingers	favorite
high	heard	garden	hesitated
here	rather	doubted	prepared
what	letters	bounded	exclaimed
full	never	prancing	unexpected
your	relieve	trundling	nevertheless

LESSON LXVIII.
More about George Washington.

1. "It is *rather wonderful*," said Mr. Washington.

2. "Ah, father, I guess," said George, looking up rather inquisitively.

3. "Well, and what do you guess, my son?"

4. "Why, I guess somebody did this. Yes, I've just thought, somebody

sowed the seed to make my name. I guess *you* did it, father, didn't you?"

5. "Well, George, for once you are quite right in your guessing. I *did* do it."

6. "What for, father?"

7. "What for! Why, does it not look beautiful?"

8. "Yes, but you had some design, father. What did you mean by it?"

9. "I meant, George" replied Mr. Washington, "by means of it to teach you an *important lesson.*"

10. "What, father, to plant seeds?"

11. "More important than that. I want to prove to you that there is a great God."

12. "Why, I believe that now, father. Mother has often told me about that."

13. "Well, but, George, how do you *know* that there is a God?"

14. "Because mother says there is."

15. "But what I mean, my son, is, how you would *prove* that there is a God?"

16. "I never studied that, father, and I don't know."

17. "Well, that is the very point which I want you to know. Listen and I will explain.

18. "A short time ago, you discovered these letters in this bed. They appeared wonderful, you called me, you wished to know how they came here. I told you they might have come by chance but this did not satisfy you. Can you tell me why?"

19. "Because it seemed as if somebody must have sowed the seed here just so," said George.

20. "True, it does appear so. Now can you tell, my son, *why* it appears so?"

21. "Because," said George. "I think somebody had a *design* in it, and you told me that *you* had some design in it, father."

22. "Just so, George, I *had* a design in it, and the *marks of design* prove that the plants did not grow that way by chance, but that some agent, or being, was concerned in them. Is it not so?"

23. "Yes, sir."

24. "Now, then, George, look around. You see this beautiful world. You see how nicely all things are planned, what marks of design there are! We have fire to warm us when we are cold, water to drink when we are thirsty, teeth to eat with, eyes to see with, feet to walk with.— In a thousand things we see design. There must, then, have been a *designer*—some one who formed these things for a *purpose*—for some *end.*"

25. "Ah!" said George, "I know whom you mean, father."

26. "Whom, my son?"

27. "God Almighty. Do you not?"

28. "Yes, I mean Him. It was He that created all the beautiful and convenient things which you see around you. I mean Him who is God the Lord, and owner of all things, and Who should be worshipped by us all."

29. "But, father, is not this garden yours, and the house, and all things around us, here?"

30. "No, my son," replied Mr. Washington, "they are not mine. True,

I call them mine, and they are mine to use, rather than my neighbor's; but they are only entrused to my care. All things belong to God. He created them, and they are His. He has given the care of them to His creatures here, and will one day require an account of them."

31. "But, father," said George, "you built your house, didn't you; and is it not yours, then?"

32. "Yes, George, but if I did build it, did I create the materials of it? Who made the trees, from which the timber, the boards, and the shingles, were obtained? From what source did the iron come, from which the nails were made? God formed all. It was He, too, who formed the oxen, and the horses, and the sheep, and everything which you see on the farm."

33. George now became silent, and appeared for a time lost in the reflections of his own mind. A good impression had been made. He seemed to feel the force of his father's remarks. From this time, it is believed, he never

doubted that there is a God, the author and proprietor of all things.

———————◆———————

Questions.—1. Who did George Washington think placed the seed in the ground? 2. What did Mr. Washington intend to teach George by it? 3. Do we not see the evidences all around us, that there is a Great Being who has made the work? 4. Aren't the things which are made, well adapted to our happiness? 5. What should this teach us of the character of that Great Being? 6. If He is good, should we not love Him? 7. What other and surer evidence have we that there is a God, than what we find in nature?

guess	marks	guessing	convenient
once	lesson	Almighty	worshipped
chance	sowed	beautiful	impression
some	design	somebody	reflections
wild	appear	appeared	proprietor
world	looking	important	Washington
look	explain	materials	

LESSON LXIX.
Father William.

1. You are old, Father William,
        Theophilus cries,
   The few locks which are left you
        are gray—
   You appear, Father William, a
        healthy old man;
   Now tell me the reason, I pray.

2. When I was a youth, Father
        William replied,
   I remembered that youth
        would fly fast;
   I abused not my health and my
        vigor at first,
   That I never might need them
        at last.

3. You are old, Father William,
        Theophilus said,
   And pleasures, with youth pass
        away;
   And yet you repent not the days
        that are gone;—
   Now tell me the reason, I pray.

4. When I was a youth, Father
William replied,
I remembered that youth could
not last;
I thought of the future, whatever
I did,
That I never might grieve for the
past.

5. You are old, Father William,
the young man still cries,
And life is swift hastening away;
You are cheerful, and love to
converse upon death!
Come tell me the reason, I pray!

6. I am cheerful, young man, Father
William replied;
Let the cause your attention
engage;
In the days of my youth I
remembered my God!
And he hath not forgotten my
age.

Questions.—1. Who is it that speaks to
Father William? 2. What does he wish to

know? 3. How had the old gentleman preserved his health so well? 4. How do we abuse our health? 5. Why was Father William so cheerful? 6. What does it mean to remember God?

death	appear	cheerful	Theophilus
young	healthy	converse	attention
youth	engage	William	forgotten
vigor	abused	measures	whatever
reason	replied	attentive	remembered
away			

LESSON LXX.
Robbing Birds' Nests.

1. A little boy who had discovered a bird's nest in a thicket was much pleased at finding such a prize. Tearing it from the place where the careful birds had placed it, he hurried away with it, rejoicing at his good fortune.

2. As he walked towards home, he met his sisters, who, when they saw the nest, explained to their brother how curiously it was formed. Moss, hair, and wool, were combined together, and these were lined with feathers by the

industrious and tender parents, to provide for the warmth and safety of their young.

3. "Do you think," said his sisters, "that any little boy has skill enough to make so wonderful a thing? There had the mother sat for days, brooding over her eggs, before the warmth called the little creatures into life.

4. "Now, as a reward of all her care, she finds her house and her little ones snatched away from her. Who can describe her distress when she returns to feed her helpless little ones and spread over them her sheltering wings! How will she complain, in a mournful song, or the injustice and cruelty of the boy who has robbed her of all that was dear to her!"

5. While the little boy looked at the nest and the young birds, and heard these remarks of his sisters, his heart was touched—he yielded to the sweet impulse of humanity. He turned around. His steps were pleasant, for he was going to amend his fault.

6. He replaced the nest in the best way he could, where he had found it, and enjoyed more satisfaction from this act of humanity, than any amusement could ever give.

7. I hope all my little readers will try to remember this story, and when they are tempted to rob birds' nests think how much better they will feel to let them alone.

───────◆◆◆───────

Questions.—1. Who was it that found a bird's nest?   2. Who met him as he was carrying it away?   3. What did they say to him?   4. Wasn't this true, and a very affecting appeal to his better feelings?   5. What did the little boy decide to do?   6. Are we not too likely to forget that animals can suffer in feeling as well as we!

moss	robbed	described	execution
sweet	reward	complain	industrious
feet	yielded	remember	satisfaction
faults	provide	explained	oppression
bestow	distress	contained	amusement
touched	towards	humanity	discovered
finding	behold	together	sheltering

LESSON LXXI.

A Dialogue on Dress.

1. *Charlotte.* Have you seen Jane, lately?

2. *Nancy.* Not since last spring, I believe.

3. *Charlotte.* You did not go to the fair, then?

4. *Nancy.* No, Mary was ill that day, and mama could not very well spare me. What were you going to say about Jane?

5. *Charlotte.* Why, that the girl has some strange ideas lately.

6. *Nancy.* Well, but what has she done? You make me impatient.

7. *Charlotte.* She won't have a new dress, or even a new bonnet this spring, she says; although her papa when he went to New York, offered to get her anything she wanted.

8. *Nancy.* Won't have things? What does she mean?

9. *Charlotte.* She has decided to dress plainly, and give what she can save to the Juvenile Industry Society,

to enable them to make or buy clothing for poor children. She seems to be resolute in her plan, for she was at the fair, last Thursday, in her old dress and old bonnet.

10. *Nancy.* The foolish Jane! The poor children of the parish might go without clothes, before I'd do that. Turn Quaker? Yes, a beautiful miss, of ten years old, go dressed like an old Quaker woman of sixty? That's a pretty affair, Charlotte.

11. *Charlotte.* But there must be something pleasant, after all, Nancy, in helping to clothe poor children. Besides, Jane's dress is *good* enough—

12. *Nancy.* Good enough! Who doesn't know that? But how I would feel to see all the girls in their new dress, and myself in my old one, especially when everybody knows that papa is as able to get new things for his children as other people are for theirs.

13. *Charlotte.* And how do the poor *children* feel, do you think, when the weather is very cold, and they have little or no clothing?

14. *Nancy.* Rich people should take care of that.

15. *Charlotte.* But will they, Nancy? Don't we see poor families suffering every day, with rich people all around them? Mrs. Carey's children—think of them!

16. *Nancy.* Oh! I know they suffer, but shall I deny myself new clothes, and be unfashionable and old womanish, to help them?

17. *Charlotte.* Ask yourself what you would wish them to do, if they were in your circumstances, and you in theirs? That will settle the question.

Questions.—1. What did Charlotte ask Nancy? 2. Why didn't Mary go to the fair? 3. What did Charlotte say Mary would not have? 4. Why did she not want it? 5. Was Nancy pleased at Mary's conduct? 6. Which was the best friend to the poor children? 7. Ought we to be extravagant in dress, and not relieve the poor?

Jane	Nancy	children	Charlotte
poor	warrant	society	Thursday
fair	woman	beautiful	suffering

dress	helping	families	fashionable
parish	bonnet	clothing	womanish
lately	offered	juvenile	especially
myself	Quaker	industry	circumstances

LESSON LXXII.

Story about Lafayette.

1. General Lafayette was a native of France. He was a young man of vast fortune and high rank. At a very early age, he took a deep interest in the affairs of America.

2. He had heard of the struggles of our ancestors in the War of Independence. When he learned of their trials and sufferings, his noble spirit was stirred within him, and he immediately determined to come to our aid.

3. He went to the American Agents in Paris and requested passage to America, but they were obliged to confess they did not have the means of sending him.

4. "Then," said he, "I will fit out a ship myself," and he did so. At the time of his arrival the prospects of our country were very dark, but when it was known that Lafayette had come with arms and money, the spirits of our troops revived.

5. Young Lafayette was welcomed by General Washington, and invited to stay in his tent. He was immediately offered a command in the American army. This he refused. He chose rather to enter as a volunteer; to raise a body of men, and clothe them at his own expense.

6. Two years after this, he was again appointed to command. He now accepted the office of Major General. He fought by the side of Washington, and shed his blood to secure for us the blessings we now enjoy.

7. When the war was over, Lafayette returned to his native land. He had cheerfully spent his time and fortune for our good. The only reward he wanted was to know we had secured our liberties.

8. After a great many years, Lafayette was invited to come again to America. The people wanted to show to him that they loved him, and were grateful for what he had done for us.

9. In 1824, he came again to America, and he was everywhere received with the greatest joy.

10. He had now become old, and most of those whom he had known were gone to their graves, but he found that in the hearts of their children, their gratitude still lived.

11. He went through the length and breadth of the land. Wherever he came

he found multitudes waiting to receive him. Each one wanted to take him by the hand, and exclaim "Welcome, welcome, thrice welcome Lafayette."

12. Lafayette was often moved to tears at these marks of gratitude, which he everywhere met. After spending one year with us, delighted with his visit, he returned again to his native France, followed by the good wishes and prayers of grateful America.

———————————

Questions.—1. What is this story about? 2. Who was Lafayette? 3. Why did he wish to come to America? 4. How was he received by General Washington? 5. What did Lafayette do after he arrived? 6. When did he return to his native land? 7. Why was he asked again to visit America?   8. Did the people show that they were grateful for the services he had rendered us?

invited   America   gratitude   multitudes
arrived   followed   Lafayette   Washington
General   wherever   sufferings   immediately

LESSON LXXIII.

Story about Joseph.

1. Jacob had twelve sons. One of them was the son of his old age. He loved him very much, and he made for him a coat of many colors; his name was Joseph.

2. And Joseph dreamed, that while he was in the field with his brothers, binding sheaves, his sheaf arose, and stood upright, and that all his brothers' sheaves bowed to his.

3. He dreamed again, and he thought that the sun and moon, and eleven stars, bowed to him.

4. He told these dreams to his father and to his brothers. His father rebuked him, and said, "Shall I, and your mother, and your brothers, indeed, come to bow down ourselves to you, to the earth?"

5. And his brothers said, "Shall you indeed reign and have dominion over us?" And they hated him even more for his dreams.

6. One day, when he came to them, as they were keeping their flocks in the field, they took him, and sold him for a slave to some merchants who were going down into Egypt. They sold him to one of the king's officers in Egypt.

7. While he was in this great man's house, he was falsely accused and thrown into prison.

8. Soon after this, Pharaoh, the king of Egypt, had a very remarkable dream, and no one could tell him the meaning of it. He was very much troubled on account of it.

9. The chief butler of the king told him that there was a young man in the prison who would explain his dream to him. He said, he knew that Joseph could, because he had explained a dream which he had when he was in prison, and that things had come to pass just as Joseph said they would.

10. Pharaoh sent for Joseph, and the great God told him what the dream meant, and he explained to the king.

11. The king said to him, "See! I have set you over all the land of

Egypt." And he made him ride in the second chariot which he had; and they cried before him, "Bow the knee!" He made Joseph ruler over all the land of Egypt.

12. His father, Jacob, who loved him so much, did not know what had become of him. Indeed his brothers, when they had sold him, took his pretty coat of many colors, and dipped it in blood. Then they showed it to his father, and told him that some wild beast had torn Joseph to pieces.

13. After some time there was a great famine in the land where Jacob lived, and as there was plenty of corn in Egypt, he sent his sons to buy some for food.

14. Joseph knew them, though they did not know him. He treated them as spies. They said that they were not, that they were all the sons of one father, and that they had left their brother Benjamin at home.

15. Joseph said, that he would know that they were what they said, if they would bring their younger brother with

them the next time they came. He kept one of them until they should do as he had said.

Questions.—1. Who had twelve sons? 2. What are they called in the Scriptures? 3. What did Joseph dream? 4. What was the meaning of these dreams? 5. How did his brothers feel towards him? 6. What did they do with him? 7. Was this an act of great cruelty? 8. Where was he carried? 9. What did they tell their father? 10. When persons begin to do wrong is it easy for them to stop? 11. How was Joseph treated in Egypt?

shalt	twelve	sheaves	brethren
colors	dreams	explain	dominion
hated	dipped	denied	rebuked
lived	plenty	chariot	meaning
butler	famine	become	merchants
prison	reaping	binding	remarkable
pretty	treated	younger	Pharaoh

LESSON LXXIV.
More about Joseph.

1. Now Jacob was very unwilling to let Benjamin go, for since he had believed that Joseph was dead, he had loved Benjamin more.

2. But at last, as they were without food, he consented. He said, "Go into Egypt again, and carry a present to the man, a little balm, and a little honey, spices and myrrh, nuts and almonds. Take also your bother, and God Almighty give you mercy before the man, that he may send away your other brother, and Benjamin. If I am bereaved of my children, I am bereaved."

3. And so they went, and they bowed themselves before Joseph to the earth. He said, "Is your father well—the old man of whom you spoke—is he still alive?"

4. Fixing his eyes on Benjamin, he said, "Is this your younger brother of whom you spoke to me?" And he said, "God be gracious to you, my son!"

5. He made himself known to his brothers. And he said, "I am Joseph, your brother, whom you sold into Egypt. Be not grieved or angry with yourselves that you sold me; for God sent me before you to preserve life."

6. He fell upon his brother Benjamin's neck, and wept; and Benjamin wept upon his neck. He kissed all his brothers, and wept upon them. "You shall tell my father," said he, "of all my glory in Egypt, and of all that you have seen; and you shall hurry and bring my father here."

7. They went back into the land of Canaan, where their father lived, and they told him that Joseph was alive, and governor over all the land of Egypt. They repeated all the words which Joseph had said to them.

8. Jacob's heart fainted within him. He thought that it was too good news to be true, and he did not believe them.

9. When, however, he saw the wagons which Joseph had sent to carry him down into Egypt, his spirit revived. He said, "It is enough; Joseph, my son, is yet alive. I will go and see him before I die!"

10. This he did, and all his family, amounting to seventy persons, went with him.

11. Joseph heard that he was coming, and he made ready his chariot, and went to meet him, and he fell on his neck, and he wept on his neck a good while. Jacob said, "Now let me die, since I have seen your face, and you art still alive!"

12. In this world our friends and our parents die. They go away from us, and we see them no more. Here we all suffer much pain and trouble.

13. There is a land where there is no affliction. There no one is sick, or dies. Our best friend—the Lord Jesus—who died for us on the cross, lives there. He is the Lord and ruler of that happy land. He will send His holy angels to bring all those who love Him, to live with Him forever.

Questions.—1. What was Jacob unwilling to do? 2. Did he finally consent? 3. To whom did Joseph make himself known? 4. How did he meet them? 5. How would most persons have treated them, after being torn from their father as he was? 6. To whom did they return? 7. Where did Jacob go? 8. What good resulted from Joseph's being sold in Egypt?   9. Did this lessen the guilt of the brothers?   10. Doesn't God overrule the purposes of the wicked?

since	wagon	grieved	Benjamin
myrrh	within	fainted	Almighty
eyes	fixing	brethren	governor
wept	Jacob	preserve	affliction
angles	Joseph	brother	believed
spirit	Egypt	present	however
before	Jesus	Canaan	amounting

LESSON LXXV.
The Obedient Casabanca.

1. There was a little boy, about thirteen years old, whose name was Casabanca. His father was the commander of a ship of war called the Orient. The little boy accompanied his father to the seas. His ship was once engaged in a terrible battle on the river Nile.

2. In the middle of the thunders of the battle, while the shot were flying thickly around, and strewing the decks with blood, this brave boy stood by the side of his father, faithfully discharging the duties which were assigned to him.

3. At last his father placed him in a particular part of the ship, to perform some service, and told him to remain at his post until he should call him away. As the father went to some distant part of the ship, to notice the progess of the battle, a ball from the enemy's vessel laid him dead upon the deck.

4. The son, unconscious of his father's death, and faithful to the trust reposed in him, remained at his post, waiting for his father's orders. The battle raged dreadfully around him. The blood of the slain flowed at his feet. The ship took fire, and the threatening flames drew nearer and nearer.

5. Still this noble-hearted boy would not disobey his father. In the face of blood, and balls, and fire, he stood firm and *obedient*. The sailors began to desert the burning and sinking ship, and the boy cried out, "Father, may I go?"

6. No voice of permission could come from the mangled body of his lifeless

father, and the boy, not knowing that he was dead, would rather die than disobey. There that boy stood, at his post, until every man had deserted the ship, and he stood and perished in the flames.

7. Oh, what a boy was that! Everybody who ever heard of him thinks that he was one of the noblest boys that ever was born. Rather than disobey his father, he would die in the flames!

8. This account has been written in poetry; and, as the children who read this book may like to see it, I will present it to them.

CASABANCA.

1. The boy stood on the burning deck,
   Whence all but him had fled;
   The flame that lit the battle's wreck,
   Shone round him over the dead.

2. Yet beautiful and bright he stood,
   As born to rule the storm;
   A creature of heroic blood,
   A proud, though childlike form.

3. The flames rolled on; he would
                              not go,
  Without his father's word;
That father, faint in death below,
  His voice no longer heard.

4. He called aloud—"Say, father, say
  If yet my task is done."
He knew not that the chieftain lay
  Unconscious of his son.

5. "Speak, father," once again he
                              cried,
  "If I may yet be gone."
And—but the booming shot replied,
  And fast the flames rolled on.

6. Upon his brow he felt their breath,
  And in his waving hair;
And looked from that lone post of
                              death,
  In still, yet brave despair;

7. And shouted but once more aloud,
  "My father, must I stay?"
While o'er him fast, through sail
                              and shroud,
  The wreathing fires made way.

8. They wrapped the ship in
                    splendor wild,
    They caught the flag on high,
    And streamed above the gallant
                    child,
    Like banners in the sky.

9. Then came a burst of thunder
                    sound—
    The boy—oh, where was he?
    Ask of the winds, that far around
    With fragments strewed the sea.

10. With mast, and helm, and
                    pennon fair,
    That well had borne their part;
    But the noblest thing that
                    perished there,
    Was that young, faithful heart.

Questions.—1. What is this story
about? 2. Who was Casabanca? 3. By
whose side did he stand in the middle of
battle? 4. What happened to his father? 5.
What took fire? 6. What did the sailors
begin to do? 7. What did the little boy
do? 8. Why did he stand there amid so

much danger?   9. What became of him?   10.
For what trait of character was he
admired?   11. What is it that makes children
lovely?

seas	father	progress	permission
river	remains	knowing	obedient
should	distant	children	Casabanca
battle	waiting	account	remained
flying	rather	disobey	particular

LESSON LXXVI.
The Lost Nestlings.

1. "Have you seen my darling
                          nestlings?"
   A mother robin cried.
   "I cannot, cannot find them,
      Though I've sought them far
                          and wide.

2. "I left them well this morning,
      When I went to seek their food;
   But I found, upon returning,
      I'd a nest without a brood.

3. "Oh, have you naught to tell me,
      That will ease my aching breast,
   About my tender offspring
      That I left within the nest?

4. "I have called them in the bushes,
   And the rolling stream beside,
Yet they came not at my bidding;
   I'm afraid they all have died!"

5. "I can tell you all about them,"
   Said a little wanton boy,
"For 'twas I that had the pleasure
   Your nestlings to destroy.

6. "But I did not think their mother
   Her little ones would miss,
Or ever come to hail me
   With a wailing sound like this.

7. "I did not know your bosom
   Was formed to suffer woe,
And mourn your murdered children,
   Or I had not grieved you so.

8. "I'm sorry that I've taken
   The lives I can't restore,
And this regret shall teach me
   To do the thing no more.

9. "I ever shall remember
   The plaintive sounds I've heard,
Nor kill another nestling
   To pain a mother bird."

Questions. —1. What is this poetry about? 2. What is a nestling? 3. By whom had they been left? 4. How did she feel when she found they were gone? 5. Who had taken them? 6. Do you think it right to cause so much distress to a bird? 7. What did this little boy determine he would never do?

robin	bosom	wanton	plaintive
rolling	afraid	nestling	remember
aching	stream	bidding	another
regret	breast	grieved	murdered
formed	brood	mother	children

LESSON LXXVII.

Story about Columbus.

1. About three hundred and fifty years ago, there lived a wise man named Columbus. He was born in Genoa, a city of Italy, in Europe.

2. Columbus believed that men could sail around the world in a ship, and come back to the place from which they started. He thought, if some people would try to do this, they would find some new country, which the people in Europe had never heard of or seen.

3. At that time, Europe, Asia, and Africa, were known and they all lie on one side of the globe. What was on the other side, none of the people in Europe could tell. Columbus wanted very much to sail over the wide sea to try to find out. But he could not go unless he had ships and men.

4. He asked the king of his country if he would get men and money and ships, and let him go—but he would not. He then applied to the king of England, and then to the king of Portugal but none would help him.

5. At last, he went to Spain. The name of the king of Spain was Ferdinand, the name of the queen was Isabella. Queen Isabella was very much pleased with the plan of Columbus. She hoped he would find the countries he expected to find, and she tried very hard to persuade the king to give Columbus the things he wanted.

6. The king promised to send Columbus, if he would agree to give him the greater part of the valuable things he might discover. Columbus

said he would do this. The king then gave him three ships, and what he wanted besides.

7. In August, 1492, the ships sailed. A great many people went to see them go. They felt very curious to know where they would go, and what new country they would find. When the sailors got far out of the sight of land, they began to be afraid. They wanted to go back to Spain, and refused to obey Columbus. Columbus persuaded them to have patience, and wait a few days.

8. In a few weeks after they left Spain, they came in sight of the Bahama Islands, and soon after, they came to larger islands, now called Cuba and St. Domingo. The people they found were not white, like the men of Europe, nor black, like those who live in Africa. The people were much frightened when they first saw Columbus with his people.

9. After a while Columbus went back to Spain. The king and queen were very glad when they heard of the new

country he had found. They sent him back again, with many other ships, and soon they found the islands now called the West Indies, and the large country of South America.

10. The Spaniards took these countries for their own, and everything they could find in them. They found a great deal of gold and silver. They treated the natives of the country very cruelly, in hopes that they would tell them of still more gold and silver than they had found.

———————

Questions.—1. What is this story about? 2. Where was Columbus born? 3. What did he wish to do? 4. What kings would not assist him? 5. What did the king of Spain do for Columbus? 6. What land did Columbus first discover? 7. What did he discover on his second voyage? 8. How did the Spaniards treat the natives of South America?

Indies	Africa	promised	Europe
Cuba	Genoa	Columbus	England
Asia	wanted	America	cruelty
much	money	Domingo	hundred
hopes	country	Spaniards	believed
found	patience	Ferdinand	curious
globe	greater	frightened	applied

LESSON LXXVIII.

Settlement of America.

1. After the discoveries of Columbus, the kings and people of other countries sent out ships to America, until in time, it was all known to the people of Europe. People came from different countries of Europe to different parts of America.

2. They found no towns and pleasant fields and fine gardens; they found only woods, and wild men, and wild animals. The men they called Indians, because they looked a little like the people who live in India, a country in Asia. There were a great many Indians then, but now there are very few.

3. As the white people increased, the Indians were driven away or killed—often with rum. The Spaniards were not only cruel to the poor Indians, but cruel to Columbus, who discovered America. They put him in prison, and let him die of want.

4. After this, many people came over from Europe to live in America. In the year 1607, they came from England

and settled at Jamestown, in Virginia. The Indians killed many. The settlers had many hardships to endure, and in six months, only a few men were left out of six hundred.

5. Many went to New England to live. Pennsylvania was settled by Swedes in 1627, and William Penn came here in 1681. He came to this country, and a great many more who were Quakers came with him because they could not worship God in their own country.

6. Very little good ever comes from fighting, and William Penn did not wish to fight with the Indians and take their land from them, though the king of England had granted it to him. He came without any army, and a great many Indian chiefs met under a large elm tree near Philadelphia.

7. He bought as much land from them as he wanted. This was much better than to try to drive them away or kill them, or make them drunk with whisky, and then cheat them, as many white men have since done.

8. Many of the first settlers in some parts of our country died of hunger, and more were murdered by the Indians. All had much suffering to endure. Then the dark forests covered the land, and the savage Indians hunted the deer and danced around their fires, and sang their songs of war.

9. We can now look around on our rich cultivated sunny hills, covered with pasture and waving with golden grain. We live in splendid cities. Beautiful villages are spread over our country, thick as the stars in an evening sky.

10. After our fathers had passed through a great many trials, and the Lord blessed their labors and smiled upon them, there were some who envied them, and the king of England began to oppress them. There were many good people in England who loved the Americans, and who did not wish to do them any harm.

11. There were others there who did not know or care anything about our

country, and thought the people here were almost the same as Indians.

———————

Questions.—1. How was America first settled?   2. Why were the natives of America called Indians?   3. What was the first settlement in North America?   4. What has been our treatment of the Indians?   5. What did William Penn do?   6. What did our forefathers endure?   7. Who brought them through their trials and protected them?

Lord	Swedes	Quakers	Jamestown
much	whisky	increase	hardships
many	without	Virginia	beautiful
prison	wanted	William	cultivated
killed	settlers	villages	murdered
passed	hunger	evening	Philadelphia
envied	hunted	covered	Pennsylvania

LESSON LXXIX.
Thoughts at Sunset.

1. The sun has gone to rest,
    The bee forsakes the flower,
  The bird hurries to its nest
    Within the leafy bower.

2. Where have I been this day?
    Into what follies run?
Forgive me, Father, when I pray
    Through Jesus Christ thy Son.

3. When all my days are over
    And in my tomb I rest,
Oh, may my happy spirit soar
    Up to a Savior's breast.

———

Questions.—1. What has gone to rest? 2. Does the sun go down, or does the earth turn around? 3. When our days on earth are spent, where can we hope to go?

flower   follies   Savior   forgive
within   Jesus

LESSON LXXX.
George and Charles.

1. George and Charles lived in the same town. They were smart boys, and both belonged to respectable families and received a good education.

2. George and Charles were both beloved by their parents and all their friends. Indeed, they were handsome boys, and they grew up into life with every prospect of usefulness.

3. They had pleasant families, and all seemed happy about them. When they were children, their fathers would invite friends to drink, and then give the boys the sugar in the bottom of the glass.

4. In this way they learned to love strong drink, and when they grew up, they drank liquor every day. When they went into company with their young friends, they were sure to drink freely.

5. As they prospered in business, they saw more company, and drank more and more, until they found the bad habit set, and they could not shake it off.

6. Now they were often seen at the whisky stores, and at the tavern. They began to neglect their business, and their customers left them, and went elsewhere to trade.

7. Their lovely wives, who used to greet them home with a smile, now grew pale and sickly. They were worn out with fatigue and sorrow.

8. Their handsome houses were soon exchanged for miserable huts, hardly sufficient to shelter them from the storm. Their property is wasted, their children are ragged and ignorant.

9. When they go home, they fill their bottles with whisky or rum, and are seen to stagger through mud and filth as they pass along. At home they meet their weeping wives and starving children, only to abuse them.

10. This is the life they lead, and surely it is a life of misery. Once these boys were happy and cheerful, but now they are disgraced even below the animals.

11. All this misery flows from what? From the use of alcoholic drinks. Alas! How many have been ruined in the same way.

12. My little readers, I have told you this very painful story, that you may

see what an awful and wicked thing it is to drink whisky, or anything that will make people drunk.

13. I hope that all little boys and girls will feel that it is a great blessing to have good parents and kind teachers, who will be dutiful to them, and keep them from running into bad habits.

———————

Questions.—1. What two boys lived in the same town? 2. By whom were they beloved? 3. Were they good boys? 4. What evil habits did they fall into? 5. What effect did it have upon them? 6. How were they taught to love whisky? 7. Wasn't this very cruel? 8. What effect did this evil habit have upon their wives? 9. What effect upon their children? 10. What must we do to escape this misery?

wives	indeed	whisky	disgraced
smile	bottles	readers	ignorant
brutes	ragged	misery	company
stores	forsook	property	prospered
surely	habits	families	usefulness
below	fixed	children	customers

LESSON LXXXI.
Things to Remember.

1. Remember, child, remember,
   That God is in the sky,
   That He looks on all we do
   With an ever wakeful eye.

2. Remember, oh, remember,
   That all the day and night,
   He sees our thoughts and actions,
   With an ever watchful sight.

3. Remember, child remember,
   That God is good and true;
   That He wishes us to be
   Like Him in all we do.

4. Remember that He hates
   A falsehood or a lie—
   Remember, He will punish
   The wicked by-and-by.

5. Remember, oh, remember,
   That He is like a friend,
   And He wishes us to be
   Good, and happy in the end.

6. Remember, child, remember,
   To pray to Him in heaven;
   And if you have done wrong,
   Oh, ask to be forgiven.

7. Be sorry, in your little prayers,
   And whisper in His ear;
   Ask His forgiveness and His love,
   And He will surely hear.

8. Yes, He will hear you and forgive
   Like a father, good and kind;
   So remember, child, remember,
   That you love with all your mind—

9. The God, who lives in heaven,
   And gives us each delight,
   Who guards us all the day,
   And saves us in the night.

———————

Questions.—1. Who is it that looks on all we do?   2. Can God see us in the dark? 3. What does God hate?   4. What must we remember to do, if we have done wrong? 5. Who will forgive us?   6. Whom must we love with all our hearts?

forgive	father	delight	watchful
wishes	heaven	actions	remember

LESSON LXXXII.
A Ship in a Storm.

1. Did you ever go far out upon the great ocean? How beautiful is it to be out at sea, when the sea is smooth and still!

2. Let a storm approach, and the scene is changed. The heavy black clouds appear in the distance, and throw a deep, death-like shade over the world of waters.

3. The captain and sailors soon see in the clouds the signs of evil. All hands are then set to work to take in sail.

4. The hoarse notes of the captain, speaking through his trumpet, are echoed from lip to lip among the rigging. Happy will it be if all is made snug before the gale strikes the vessel.

5. At last it comes, like a vast moving mountain of air. It strikes the ship, the vessel heaves and groans under the dreadful weight, and struggles to escape through the foaming waters!

6. If she is far out at sea, she will be likely to ride out the storm in safety, but if the wind is driving her upon the shore, the poor sailors will hardly escape being dashed upon the rocks and drowned.

7. In the picture you can see a ship in a storm. You can see that some of her masts are already broken, and her sails lost.

8. While the wind was raging, and the billows dashed against her, the cry was heard—"A man has fallen overboard!"

9. Quickly the boat was lowered, and she was soon seen bounding her way over the mountain waves.

10. At one moment the boat seemed lifted to the skies, and the next moment she sank down and appeared to be lost beneath the waves.

11. At length the man was found. He was almost drowned; but he was taken on board, and now they made for the ship.

12. The ship rolled so dreadfully, that it seemed certain destruction to go near her. Now what should they do?

13. The captain directed one of the men to go aloft and throw down a rope. This was made fast to the boat, and when the sea favored, she was hoisted up, and all fell into the ship with a dreadful crash!

14. It was a desperate way of getting on board, but providentially no lives were lost.

15. All in all, a sailor's life is a very hard life. Our young friends owe a debt of gratitude to those whose home is upon the great waters, and who bring

them the luxuries of other countries.

16. Good men have built many chapels for seamen on shore. A great deal has been done for them, that their stay on shore may be pleasant and profitable.

———————————

Questions.—1. What is this story about? 2. When is it dangerous to be at sea? 3. What do the sailors then aim to do? 4. In what situation are they most likely to be saved? 5. What are they doing on board of the ship in the picture? 6. Why had the boat been out? 7. Whose life is hard and dangerous?

heaves	rigging	throwing	countries
groans	echoed	distance	gratitude
weight	moving	dreadful	desperate
strikes	broken	pleasant	profitable
captain	famine	hoisted	destruction
sailors	raging	favored	dreadfully
waters	billows	directed	providentially

LESSON LXXXIII.
The Ten Commandments.

1. Every little boy and girl should know the Ten Commandments and be careful to obey them.

2. They were written by God himself, on two tables of stone. He then gave the tables to His servant Moses while he was upon Mount Sinai, amid thunders and lightnings and smoke.

3. The Ten Commandments embrace our duty to God and our neighbors. These are called the law of God.

4. All sin consists in breaking this law. Unfortunately we have all broken it, and have thus become exposed to the penalty, which says, "The soul that sinneth, it shall die."

5. But there is a way of escape from the punishment which we all deserve. The Savior has died and suffered for us. He is able and willing to save all who will seek the forgiveness of God through Him.

THE TEN COMMANDMENTS.

1. Thou shalt have no other Gods before me.

2. Thou shalt not make unto thee any graven image, or any likeness of anything that is in heaven above, or that is in the earth beneath; or that is

in the waters under the earth. Thou shalt not bow down thyself to them, nor serve them; for I the Lord thy God am a jealous God, visiting the iniquity of the fathers upon the children, unto the third and fourth generations of them that hate me, and showing mercy unto thousands of them that love me, and keep my commandments.

3. Thou shalt not take the name of the Lord thy God in vain; for the Lord will not hold him guiltless that taketh His name in vain.

4. Remember the Sabbath Day, to keep it holy. Six days shalt thou labor, and do all thy work; but the seventh day is the Sabbath of the Lord thy God; in it thou shalt not do any work, thou, nor thy son, nor thy daughter, thy man-servant, nor thy maid-servant, nor thy cattle, nor the stranger that is within thy gates; for in six days the Lord made heaven and earth, the sea, and all that in them is, and rested on the seventh day; wherefore the Lord blessed the Sabbath Day, and hallowed it.

5. Honor thy father and thy mother, that thy days may be long in the land which the Lord thy God giveth thee.

6. Thou shalt not kill.

7. Thou shalt not commit adultery.

8. Shou shalt not steal.

9. Thou shalt not bear false witness against thy neighbor.

10. Thou shalt not covet thy neighbor's house, thou shalt not covet thy neighbor's wife nor his man-servant, nor his maid-servant, nor his ox, nor his ass, nor anything that is thy neighbor's.

———————

Questions.—1. By whom were the Ten Commandments written? 2. On what were they written? 3. To whom did God give them? 4. Who was Moses? 5. Is there anything unreasonable enjoined in the Ten Commandments? 6. What punishment will God inflict upon those who break His law? 7. In prefixing this penalty hasn't God shown His desire to have us obey and be happy? 8. How can we escape from the punishment due to us? 9. Wasn't God very merciful to give His son to die for our sins? 10. Can we expect forgiveness unless we repent and break off from our sins?

wherefore   commandments   adultery
remember   punishment   thousands
neighbor   unfortunately   sabbath
guiltless   forgiveness   hallowed

LESSON LXXXIV.

About Using Profane Language.

1. All children know what is meant by profane swearing, yet, but few understand the nature and extent of the guilt incurred by it.

2. If any of you had a very dear friend who had bestowed many valuable gifts upon you, and to whom you felt the warmest gratitude, and who was entitled to your most profound respect on account of his moral excellencies of character, you would not use the name of that friend in a disrespectful manner. Nor could you hear it so used by another, without the greatest pain.

3. It would be base ingratitude in *you*, to use it lightly, and he would have little regard for your feelings, who would use it that way in your presence.

4. God has been kinder to us than *all* our earthly friends. He has given us such favors as we can never hope to return, or give to any others. Gratitude is the only return we can make.

5. He is the very *fountain* of all moral excellence, and therefore can never be sufficiently venerated. Will you then, my young reader, treat God as you would not treat a friend? There is not one among you, who could bear to be thought ungrateful. Will you therefore show more unpardonable ingratitude to your Creator, than you *can* to any relation or earthly benefactor?

6. You all know that as you become familiar with any object, however beautiful, or striking it may be, you cease to consider it as a matter of interest and importance. You could all crowd to see an exhibition of artificial fireworks, while you scarcely think of the sun—the most glorious of all fireworks—at least as an object of curiosity.

7. Now if we love our country, we must respect the name of the Deity, for the profane man can never recognize the sanctity of an oath, for the same reason that you do not feel admiration and astonishment at the sight of the sun. Then if oaths are not binding, we will have no means of eliciting truth in our courts of justice, or of binding men to a performance of duty in offices of high importance.

8. Besides all these considerations, God has given an express command, "Swear not at all." We have religion, honor, gratitude and patriotism, and *God himself*, all forbidding profanity.

———————

Questions.—1. What is the subject of this lesson? 2. What is it to swear? 3. Is it a very foolish habit? 4. Is it polite to swear? 5. Is it very wicked? 6. What is said about profane swearers in the Bible?

meant	regard	disrespectful
guilt	manners	admiration
dear	another	performance
friend	excellent	consideration
without	character	importance

profound	relative	forbidding
feelings	ungrateful	astonishment
therefore	benefactor	curiosity
greatest	sufficiently	recognize

LESSON LXXXV.

The Mother and her Child.

1. "Mother, who made the stars,
          which light
   The beautiful blue sky?
   Who made the moon, so clear and
          bright,
   That rises up on high?"

2. "Twas God, my child, the
          glorious One—
   He formed them by His power;
   He made alike the brilliant sun,
   And every leaf and flower.

3. "He made your little feet to walk;
   Your sparkling eyes to see;
   Your busy prattling tongue to talk;
   And limbs so light and free.

4. "He paints each fragrant flower
                    that blows
   With loveliness and bloom;
   He gives the violet and the rose
   Their beauty and perfume.

5. "Our various wants His hands
                    supply,
   His care protects us every hour;
   We're kept beneath His watchful
                    eye,
   And always guarded by His
                    power.

6. "Then let your little heart, my
                    love,
   Its grateful homage pay,
   To this kind Friend, who, from
                    above,
   So gently guides you every day."

———————

Questions.—1. Who is first supposed to speak in this lesson? 2. Who is it that replies? 3. What does she say is made by God? 4. What is it to pay grateful homage?

prattling	watchful	liveliness
fragrant	grateful	various
beneath	protects	brilliant

THE ECLECTIC THIRD READER,

Consisting of beautiful Selections from Prose and Poetry, with Plain Rules for Reading, and Directions for avoiding Common Errors.—By Wm. H. McGuffey, late Professor at Miami University, Oxford; now, President of Cincinnati College.

SPECIMEN OF THE THIRD READER.
LESSON XXVI.

Rules—1. Let your reading be as much as possible like good speaking or conversation.

2. Avoid reading rapidly, and carelessly, as you approach the end of a sentence.

3. On reading pieces of *this* kind, a little more animation is necessary, than in those which have preceded it.

INSIGNIFICANCE OF THE EARTH.—
CHALMERS.

1. The universe at large would suffer as little, in its splendor and variety, by the destruction of our planet, as the verdure and sublime magnificence of a forest would suffer by the fall of a single leaf.

2. The leaf quivers on the branch which supports it. It is at the mercy of the slightest accident. A breath of wind tears it from its stem, and it lands on the stream of water which passes underneath.

3. In a moment of time, the life, which we know by the microscope, it teems with is extinguished. An occurrence, so insignificant in the eye of man, and on the scale of his observation, carries in it, to the myriads which

people this leaf, an event as terrible and decisive, as the destruction of a world.

4. Now, on the grand scale of the universe, we, the occupants of this ball, which performs its little round among the suns and the systems that astronomy has unfolded, we may feel the same littleness, and the same insecurity.

5. We differ from the leaf only in this circumstance, that it would require the operation of great elements to destroy us. These elements exist. The fire which rages within may lift its devouring energy to the surface of our planet, and transform it into one wide and wasting volcano.

6. The sudden formation of elastic matter in the bowels of the earth, (and it is within the agency of known means to accomplish this,) may explode it into fragments. The exhalation of noxious air from below, may impart a virulence to the air that is around us. It may affect the delicate proportion of its ingredients, and the whole of animated nature may wither and die, under the malignity of a tainted atmosphere.

7. A blazing comet may cross the fated planet in its orbit, and realize all the terrors which superstition has conceived of it. We cannot anticipate with precision, the consequences of an event, which every astronomer must know to lie within the limits of possibility.

8. It may hurry our globe towards the sun, or drag it to the outer regions of the planetary system, or give it a new axis of revolution. The effect, which I shall simply announce, without explaining it, would be to change the place of the ocean, and bring another mighty flood upon our islands and continents.

9. These are changes which may happen in a single instant of time, and against which, nothing, known in the present system of things, provides us with any security. They might not destroy the earth, but they would unpeople it; and we who walk upon its surface with such firm and assured footsteps, are at the mercy of devouring elements, which, if let loose upon us by the hand of the Almighty, would spread solitude, and silence, and death, over the dominion of the world.

Questions.—Would the harmony of the universe be destroyed by the destruction of our earth? It is *possible* that this earth should be destroyed by natural agents? What should this teach us?

ERRORS.—*mag-nif-i-cunce*, for mag-nif-i-cence; *mic-ros-cope*, for mi-cro-scope; *as-tron-e-mer*, for as-tron-o-mer; *ex-plan-ir-to-ry*, for ex-plan-a-to-ry; *an-ni-hul-late*, for an-ni-hi-late; *a-ginst*, for a-gainst.

SPELL AND DEFINE.— (1) universe; (6) exhalations, noxious, elastic; (7) anticipate; (8) planetary; (9) destroy.

PUBLISHERS ADVERTISEMENT.

The "Eclectic Readers" have been published three months. In that time *four editions* have been disposed of, and the demand is continually increasing. The following notices among others have been received.—

From the Cincinnati Journal and Luminary.—We are sincerely pleased with this series. The works evince much care. The selections are very simple, very entertaining, and of unimpeachable morality.

"We think no school can use them without some of the following effects, viz.—great facility on the part of the teacher—great ease in understanding them, and (if the questions be adopted) great progress in learning to *think* of what they read.

They are printed in a very superior style; the paper is good and the type clear. We see no *Eastern books* with which the Eclectic Series would not compete *to great advantage.*

From the American Presbyterian, Nashville, Tenn.— Until very recently, it must be admitted that the First Books for children have been miserably defective in this one point—they have been utterly unsuited to the age and capacity of the learner.

We are therefore inclined to support and favor every attempt to remedy the evil. We have looked over two of these Books, and though we should not pretend to decide upon the whole course upon so slight an examination, yet, we have from these two, formed a favorable opinion of the "Eclectic Series," and think them as well adapted as anything we have seen to the capacity of the learners for whom they are designed. The Readers are progressive, useful in their subject matter, and written so that at each stage of its progress the young mind can grasp the whole *meaning* without too great an effort to understand the *words.*

From the Baptist Journal of the Valley of the Mississippi.—These are new works. They combine, in a high degree, the prime excellencies which should characterise Reading

Books for children and youth in our schools. They are filled with pieces easy to be understood and interesting to
the young mind. This is necessary, to fix the attention.
They furnish a rich storehouse of interesting facts on
various subjects and sound moral principles, which being
treasured up in the youthful mind, will prove of great value
in after life.

The simple easy style of the pieces, together with the
interesting matter they contain, will be highly favorable
to the formation, in the pupil, of an easy natural manner
of reading—an acquisition, which is made with difficulty
when such books as Murray's Reader, for instance, are used. We commend the Eclectic Readers to the notice of
Teachers.